Discovering Book of Mormon *Lands*

Discovering Book of Mormon *Lands*

Vaughn Hansen, Ph.D.

v.2

ISBN: 1-55517-335-7

10 9 8 7 6 5 4 3 2 1

Published and Distributed by:

CFI

Cedar Fort, Incorporated

925 North Main, Springville, Ut 84663 801-489-4084

Cover Design by Lyle Mortimer
Typeset and Page Layout by Corinne A. Bischoff
Printed in the United States of America

Table of Contents

CHAPTER SEVEN

CHAPTER EIGHT

CHAPTER NINE

CHAPTER TEN

FIGURES

ACKNOWLEDGMENTS

To many loved ones, friends, and colleagues, I gratefully express my sincere gratitude for their valued assistance; to my eternal companion of 55 years for her faith, encouragement, support, and cherished memories; to Dr. David L. Wood for his wisdom, insight, and scholarly contribution; to Dr. David S. Gailey for his sincere friendship and suggestions; to my sons Jerry and Paul and to my granddaughter Amy Wood for their assistance with the manuscript and figures; to many searchers after truth who have laid the foundation for a clearer understanding of Book of Mormon lands; and finally and most significantly to those inspired and dedicated prophets who have given us this pearl of great value, the Book of Mormon.

1

Why Search for Book of Mormon Lands?

What value lies in the knowledge of where Book of Mormon people lived, when the primary purpose of the book is to provide us with "Another Testament of Jesus Christ?" The oft-repeated spiritual message of the book is that obedience brings joy and peace, and disobedience brings unhappiness and conflict. Many people have testified, as Moroni promised, that "with a sincere heart, with real intent, having faith in Christ" the truth will be known and a testimony gained. (Moroni 10:4.)

Then why concern ourselves with the lands of the Book of Mormon? What value comes from visiting lands where their spiritual history occurred? The question can be asked of those who have been to the Garden Tomb in Jerusalem, or the Sacred Grove in New York, or the

Kirtland Temple, or the Carthage Jail, or Temple Square in Salt Lake City. Many thousands with strong testimonies visit these sacred sites each year. Were their testimonies enhanced, were their understandings increased?

With many others I can answer with a resounding yes. I have been to the Garden Tomb, to the Sacred Grove, to the Kirtland Temple, and to the Carthage Jail. I have visited Temple Square in Salt Lake City scores of times. My testimony was greatly enriched as I stood at these sacred sites. And I was likewise blessed when I stood where an ancient Nephite temple once stood. Visiting sacred sites brings a physical reality to scriptural truths recorded in sacred books.

The day is not far distant when those with testimonies will be able to visit Book of Mormon lands and be inspired and uplifted as they stand where prophets of old stood, and where the risen Christ blessed the Nephites.

Mine has been a life-long interest in the Book of Mormon, both as a solid spiritual document and also as a factual account of people and places on the American continent. Over the years, I have read, reread, and marked those passages of scripture that held special significance to me, passages that conveyed both spiritual and physical reality. During numerous journeys as a consulting engineer and as a student of the Book of Mormon, I studied local topography, maps and cultures. For more than 50 years, I have studied published accounts of efforts to identify the lands of the Book of Mormon.

My purpose in writing this book is to present to you an overview that will convey an increased reality and closeness to those ancient people and their messages contained in the book. I will not deal with specific locations of cities and temples, although some have been found. Their probable general location will be suggested in the following chapters. Different opinions exist among individuals who are intently concerned with specifics, although a consensus is rapidly evolving on the general area and major geographic features. My purpose here will be to present information upon which there is general agreement, and to identify where lack of general agreement exists. I emphasize the work "general," because in any evolving study there will always be those who disagree.

The purpose of this account is to assist the reader of the Book of Mormon to obtain a personal knowledge of it's lands and peoples and thereby to feel a closer kinship to their great prophets and their priceless messages, and to develop an increased love for the book. These were real people living in a real land with timeless counsel conveyed to you and to me.

Joseph Smith with divine assistance translated the Book of Mormon. He attested to the book's value when he said "that the Book of Mormon was the most correct of any book on earth, and the keystone of our religion, and that a man would get nearer to God by abiding by its precepts, than by any other book." (Smith, *Teachings of the Prophet Joseph Smith*, page 194.)

Ezra Taft Benson, quoting Marion G. Romney, stated that we hardly fathom the power of the book. That there is a power in the book to help us to resist temptation, to avoid deception, to stay on the straight and narrow path, and to find life in greater abundance. (Ensign, Nov. 1986, page 7.)

Moroni in about A.D. 421 recorded in the book his final testimony; "when ye shall receive these things, …if ye shall ask God with a sincere heart, with real intent, having faith in Christ, he will manifest the truth of it unto you by the power of the Holy Ghost." (Moroni 10:4.)

Thus, it behooves us not only to absorb what the Book of Mormon prophets wrote but also to obtain a personal oneness with those who experienced the events they described. To be where they were, to see what they saw, to pause and reflect where they sought guidance does enrich and deepen our understanding.

As we seek the lands where they lived, we must first accept as a foundation that the Book of Mormon is correct. Then we must understand and build upon the book's extensive content regarding the lands where the people lived. When our thinking is at variance with the statements of Mormon, we must back up and discover where we took the wrong turn.

Prior Theories and Present Consensus

A review of prior publications will not be discussed nor evaluated, because the primary essence of this publication will be the record in the Book of Mormon itself and the corresponding physical evidence. This procedure does not imply that prior research and publications have not made a contribution. Most assuredly the many dedicated authors have made significant contributions without which we would not have the general consensus that exists today. Again, my purpose is to understand better the record in the Book of Mormon itself. The book will be my primary reference, but what follows also reflects my many years of personal research, studying intently the Book of Mormon, reading the published documents, and traveling in the land.

Through the years, a general agreement about the location of Book of Mormon lands has emerged. This is progress. But many questions remain. Today most writers agree that the major lands of the Book of Mormon are in Guatemala and in Central and Southern Mexico, this area of highest ancient civilization is called Mesoamerica. Careful research based upon ever increasing knowledge has lead to this conclusion.

The thesis that Book of Mormon history occurred in both North and South America is no longer seriously considered. The record of travel in the book clearly confirms that they occupied a much smaller area.

Location of Book of Mormon Lands

Figure 1 shows where I believe the peoples of the Book of Mormon lived. Clues from the scriptures will be correlated to physical conditions in Guatemala, Belize, and the Yucatan Peninsula of southeastern Mexico. The reasons for suggesting this location will be detailed in the following chapters.

figure 1

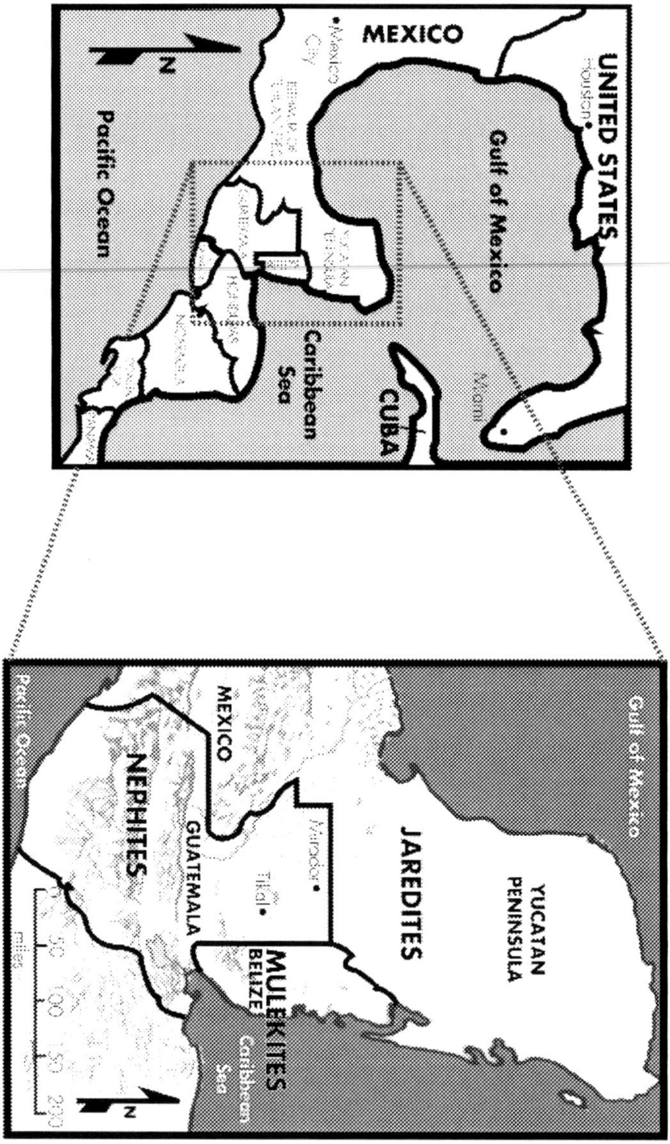

Land of the Book of Mormon in Guatemala, Belize, and Yucatan Peninsula.

My Request

I ask that you, the reader, sincerely consider the suggestions and the possibilities I here present concerning the lands of the Book of Mormon. Several of these ideas are at variance with present claims of some authors. As stated earlier, my intent is not to criticize others, but to sincerely and humbly present opinions that seem to me to be sustained by the written record in the Book of Mormon. I hope that some of these ideas will be of value to those who, with a sincere heart and with real intent, are seeking to better understand where Book of Mormon peoples lived.

2

Essentials to Finding and Understanding

This chapter consists of a listing of essential concepts needed to understand the scriptures concerning the lands of the Book of Mormon. Detailed discussions are in later chapters.

A Divinely Translated Record

The Book of Mormon must be our foundation if we are to earnestly seek and understand the land of it's people. What better foundation exists than to build upon the Prophet Joseph Smith's testimony that the book is the most correct of any book. A remarkable consistency exists throughout the book from the first (page 1) to the last (page 531), and from before 2,500 B.C. to A.D. 421. And thus it must be, since Joseph Smith translated using the

Urim and Thummim provided by the Lord, and since he had the companionship of the Holy Ghost as he translated; so Mormon also had the blessings of the Lord as he abridged the records and wrote his testimony on his own plates. We build upon a solid foundation when we accept the fact that what is written in the book is correct. However, care must be taken to avoid personal interpretations *not consistent* with the entire written record.

The computer is a marvelous tool enabling us to assemble all scripture pertaining to a specific subject, but to understand the meaning of a single verse it is often necessary to study carefully the preceding and the following verses of recorded scripture. Thus, the human tendency to select and to quote the scripture that tends to confirm personal opinion and to overlook other pertinent scripture can be reduced. One must remain teachable, seeking diligently to understand what is written.

Family History

As with the Bible, the Book of Mormon is a family history. The Bible is a history of Abraham's family, while the Book of Mormon is a history of Lehi's family. Other people with significant cultures sometimes existed not far from the "family." These other people are not mentioned in the Bible or in the Book of Mormon unless they impacted that "family." Many sincere believers in the Book of Mormon have erroneously assumed that all ancient inhabitants in the Americas and their posterity are descendants of Book of Mormon people.

Wars of annihilation occurred destroying Jaredite and also Nephite armies, governments, religious leadership, and written history. The seemingly logical, but untrue, assumption has often been made that *all* Jaredites and *all* Nephites were destroyed and that only Lamanites remained. The first fact is that other Jaredites and their descendants as well as Nehor's influence (priestcraft) persisted into Nephite times. Another fact is that the Nephite record states several thousand Nephites sailed away with Hagoth. (Alma 63:5-8.) These non-combatant Nephites undoubtedly survived.

Nephite-Lamanite History Occurred in a Small Area

The Book of Mormon clearly indicates that the entire written account occurred in a rather small area. The longest recorded journey of Nephite families with tents and livestock was 22 days between the cities of Nephi and Zarahemla, perhaps a distance of 200 to 300 miles. (Mosiah 23:3; 24:25.)

Much confusion has resulted from those who have not studied carefully the extensive geographical content of the book. They claim that both North and South America were Book of Mormon lands, and that the final battle of the Nephites and Lamanites occurred in upper New York. However, as with the Bible, the Book of Mormon stories cover a rather limited geographical area.

Present Tourist Attractions Are Not Nephite Ruins

Nephites did not build the massive stone structures the tourist sees today in Mexico and Guatemala. Archaeologists have confirmed that most of the large ruins in Mexico and Guatemala were built more than 200 years after Christ visited the Nephites. However, many structures that the tourist visits today were built over earlier structures. For example, the North Acropolis at Tikal in northern Guatemala had four stages of construction extending over a period of nearly 1500 years. Also, stages of construction are evident at Chichen Itza in the Yucatan. However, the Nephite temple sites that have been identified have not been disturbed and are still considered sacred by the local people.

The largest classic structures often contain grotesque and ugly carvings depicting gods, warriors, and rulers. Nephites did not carve images of their leaders nor portray themselves as deities, nor did they worship idols and indulge in human sacrifice. The commonly visited tourist attractions were built by pagans who worshiped Satan, he who falsely claimed to be the Son of God. Throughout time, spiritually enlightened people have never left such evidence of themselves.

Book of Mormon Was Deposited in New York State

After the final Nephite battle at Cumorah (A.D. 385), Moroni had to flee northward. His father and a few other survivors of the battle fled southward and were killed. Not until 16 years later (A.D. 401) was Moroni able to slip into the center of civil conflict around Cumorah, where the final Nephite battle had occurred; there he added a few words to the abridgement that had been made by his father Mormon. His words are some of the saddest recorded in all scripture. He was alone. Civil war still raged in the land, and he knew not how long he might be permitted to live. If captured, he would be killed. (Mormon 8:1-6.)

Finally, between A.D. 400 and 421 Moroni had enough gold to make more plates to record his abstract of the Book of Ether (the record of the Jaredites), and to add a few more things of worth. Civil war raged among the Lamanites, "and because of their hatred they put to death every Nephite that will not deny the Christ. And I, Moroni, will not deny the Christ; wherefore, I wander whithersoever I can for the safety of mine own life." (Moroni 1:1-4.)

Thus, about 36 years had passed from the time of the last Nephite battle until Moroni wrote his final words of council and his admonition to us to "ask God, the Eternal Father, in the name of Christ, if these things are not true; and if ye shall ask with a sincere heart; with real intent, having faith in Christ, he will manifest the truth of it unto you, by the power of the Holy Ghost." (Moroni 10:4.) As we seek to discover the land of the Book of Mormon, we must heed Moroni's counsel.

Two Cumorahs

Understanding that Mormon's language was Hebrew (Mormon 9:32-33) will be helpful in recognizing unique aspects of the language of the book, and thus be an aid to the study of the land. For example, nouns in Hebrew usually have meanings that sometimes vary with usage. Abram's name no longer was descriptive of the man after a remarkable interchange with the Lord. Thereafter his name was Abraham, which meant "father of many nations." (Genesis 17:5.)

And so it was with Cumorah. The Hebrew noun "Cumorah" describes this unique place as a source of light. Cumorah is a descriptive term referring to the place where sacred scriptures were deposited.

There are two Cumorahs. One hill Cumorah is where Mormon deposited sacred Nephite records, and where the final Nephite battle occurred in A.D. 385. The other Cumorah is the hill in upper New York State where Moroni deposited the abridgment of those records, the place where Joseph Smith would be in 1823. These are two separate locations. The written record clearly does not support the possibility that the final Nephite battle occurred in upper New York.

Without doubt, Moroni buried the completed record in a stone box in upper New York State, where the young prophet Joseph Smith would be in 1823. We do not know when Moroni placed the plates there, but he had at least 20 years and possibly 36 after the final Nephite-Lamanite battle before his death. He may have spent much of that time in the land to the north (likely the United States) where many thousands of Nephites had immigrated in the days of Hagoth. (Alma 63:4-7.) He may even have placed the plates in the hill Cumorah as a resurrected being.

Jaredite Hill Ramah is the Nephite Hill Cumorah

The Book of Mormon specifically states that the hill Ramah where the Jaredites were destroyed is the same hill Cumorah where the Nephites had their final battle. (Ether 15:1; Mormon 6:2.) This fact is very helpful in showing that Jaredite land is adjacent to Nephite land. Further evidence of this is found in the fact that the land the Nephites called Desolation was north of their land

Bountiful and was a land deforested by Jaredites. (Helaman 3:5-7.)

Directions in the Book of Mormon

Directions (north, south, east, and west) as well as the terms northward, eastward, and southward in the Book of Mormon are always consistent and very useful. Mormon obviously knew the country well, and Nephite prophets had the Liahona, a remarkable compass. (1 Nephi 16:10.) After receiving the Liahona, the Nephites "traveled for the space of four days, nearly a south-southeast direction." After pausing to slay food in the wilderness for their families, they "did go forth again in the wilderness, following the same direction, keeping in the most fertile parts of the wilderness, which were in the borders near the Red Sea." (1 Nephi 16:13-14.) Later they "did travel nearly eastward from that time forth...until they did come to the land which we called Bountiful" by the sea. (1 Nephi 17:1,5.)

There is only one Red Sea, referred to 28 times in the Bible, 11 times in the Book of Mormon, and twice in the Doctrine and Covenants. Travel down the east side of the Red Sea would have been in a south-southeast direction. Nephi used the same directions we use today and so did Mormon and Joseph Smith. The book *was* written for us, and when directions as stated in the book are used, a consistent layout of probable locations of lands and cities results; this will be shown in subsequent chapters.

An interesting and significant comparison of direction designations in the Bible and in the Book of Mormon is obvious in the following table.

Number of Times Scriptures are Referenced

	Book of Mormon	Bible
North	34	132
Northward	41	26
Toward the North	0	35
South	32	137
Southward	19	25
Toward the South	0	32
East	43	167
Eastward	3	43
Toward the East	0	39
West	34	167
Westward	0	27
Toward the West	0	13

In the Bible, dual terms are used: northward and toward the north, southward and toward the south, eastward and toward the east, and westward and toward the west. In the Book of Mormon, the terms northward, southward, and eastward are used. Significantly, such terms as "toward the north," "toward the south," "toward the west," or "toward the east" are *never* used. Consequently, *northward* in the Book of Mormon means either "northward" or "toward the north" as used in the Bible. Webster defines *toward* as "in the direction of."

Cardinal directions as stated in the book are critical, if we are to determine probable locations of Book of Mormon cities and lands. The fact is that the book was written for us in the latter days (2 Nephi 3:12), and was translated in modern speech by the gift and power of God, into a language *we* would understand; the translator used the Urim and Thummim, a divine instrument, that had been prepared to translate ancient records. Thus, north is north as *we* understand north. Using directions as written in the book brings clarity and consistency to the entire written record.

City to City

Consistency exists throughout the book whenever travel occurs between cities. The sequence in which cities are listed is an excellent indication of physical sequence. This fact is a significant aid in determining the approximate position of principal communities.

Up, Down, and Over

These terms are used extensively and consistently to describe travel between two locations. Thus, approximations of topography can be made. For example, travel from Zarahemla to the City of Nephi is always "up." Travel from Zarahemla to Gideon is always "over." Up, down or over are used about 88 times to describe travel between cities or lands.

Mineral Deposits

The mining of gold, silver, copper, and other minerals enhanced the wealth of both Jaredites and Nephites. (1 Nephi 18:25; 2 Nephi 5:15.) Hence, mineral-bearing rock formations must exist in these lands and can be used to locate probable Book of Mormon sites. Information obtained during a recent trip to Guatemala regarding locations of mineral deposits confirms that the lands suggested in subsequent chapters as the location of Book of Mormon lands do contain gold, silver, and other minerals as recorded in the Book of Mormon.

Seas

Seas north, south, east, and/or west are identified 23 times in the book. These geographical references are significant and will be mentioned and analyzed in later chapters.

A Narrow Pass or Passage or Neck

This physical feature is very frequently referred to in the book. An isthmus with a sea west and a sea east at the narrow pass existed between the land south and the land north before the land changes that occurred at the time of the crucifixion. This is a valuable reference. (Alma 50:34.)

Wilderness

A narrow strip of wilderness is frequently noted separating the Lamanites in the south from the Nephites in the north. The general consensus among most current Book of Mormon scholars is that the narrow strip of wilderness is in Guatemala north of the Motagua River. This narrow strip of wilderness is at the junction of two massive tectonic plates of earth. This will be further discussed in the following chapter. Also wilderness areas existed north, south, west, and east from the land of Zarahemla.

The next chapter will discuss the physical changes to the land that probably occurred at the time of the crucifixion. Then the balance of the text will show how the record in the Book of Mormon correlates with physical conditions in Guatemala, Belize, and the Yucatan Peninsula.

3

Physical Changes at the Time of the Crucifixion

Those who have attempted to identify the land of the Book of Mormon have been frustrated, because the written record clearly indicates that major changes occurred at the time of the crucifixion which drastically changed the face of the land. What changes occurred, and where did these changes occur? An understanding of these physical changes in the land is vital for an understanding of the scriptural clues to Book of Mormon lands.

When Christ was crucified, many cities were destroyed. Zarahemla burned, and Moroni sank into the sea. Moronihah was covered with earth. In all, sixteen cities were destroyed. Earthquakes, volcanic activity, tempests, and lightning were severe. (3 Nephi 8:13-17; 9:3-12.)

"And there was a great and terrible destruction in

the land southward. But behold, there was a more great and terrible destruction in the land northward; for behold, the whole face of the land was changed." (3 Nephi 8:11-12.)

Volcanic Eruptions

Physical and scriptural evidence indicates that volcanic eruptions occurred in the land southward. Ash fallout would have been extensive, and tempests and lightnings would have been severe. Similar devastation occurred when Mount St. Helens, located in the State of Washington, erupted in 1980.

Sixteen volcanic cones exist in southern Guatemala near the suggested land of Nephi. (Figure 2.) Eruption of one or more volcanoes at the time of the crucifixion would have destroyed numerous cities in the adjacent land of Nephi as recorded in 3 Nephi 8.

figure 2

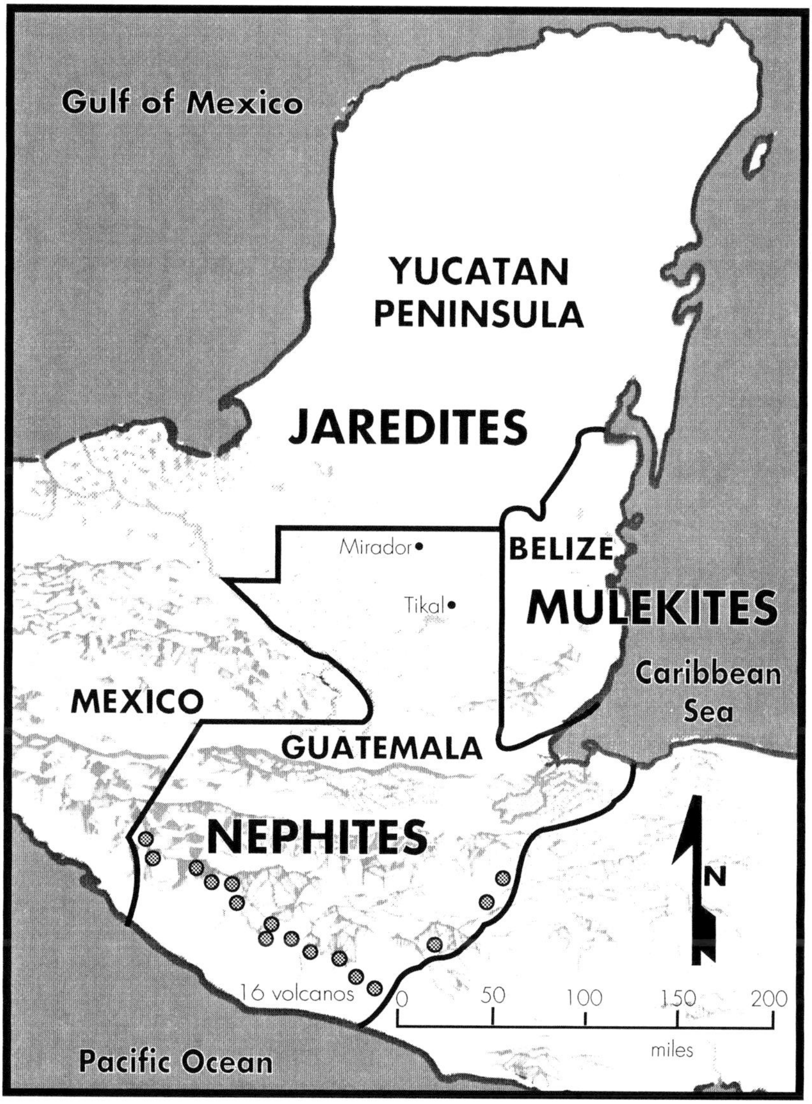

Sixteen volcanoes in the Land Southward in southern Guatemala.

Earthquakes

Much damage was done by severe earthquakes. "And the city of Moroni did sink into the depths of the sea." (3 Nephi 8:9.) "And the earth was carried up upon the city of Moronihah, that in the place of the city there became a great mountain. And there was a great and terrible destruction in the land southward." (3 Nephi 8:10-11.) More terrible destruction occurred in the land northward. The whole face of the land was changed. (3 Nephi 8:12.) "And the highways were broken up, and the level roads were spoiled, and many smooth places became rough. And many great and notable cities were sunk." (3 Nephi 8:13-14.)

The basic geologic structure of the proposed land of the Book of Mormon (Guatemala, Belize, and the Yucatan Peninsula shown in figure 1) explains why such violent destruction occurred.

Narrow Strip of Wilderness

Figure 3 shows the approximate location in Guatemala of the junction of two massive continental plates, called tectonic plates, where a narrow strip of wilderness exists. North of this massive fault extending east and west across Guatemala is the large North American Plate, which includes not only all of Mexico but also all of the United States and Canada. South of the fault is the smaller Caribbean Plate which includes the Central American countries. Several east-west faults appear on Quatemalan geologic maps to the north of the junction of the two plates. Lateral movement occurred with the north plate moving west with regard to the south plate. The

figure 3

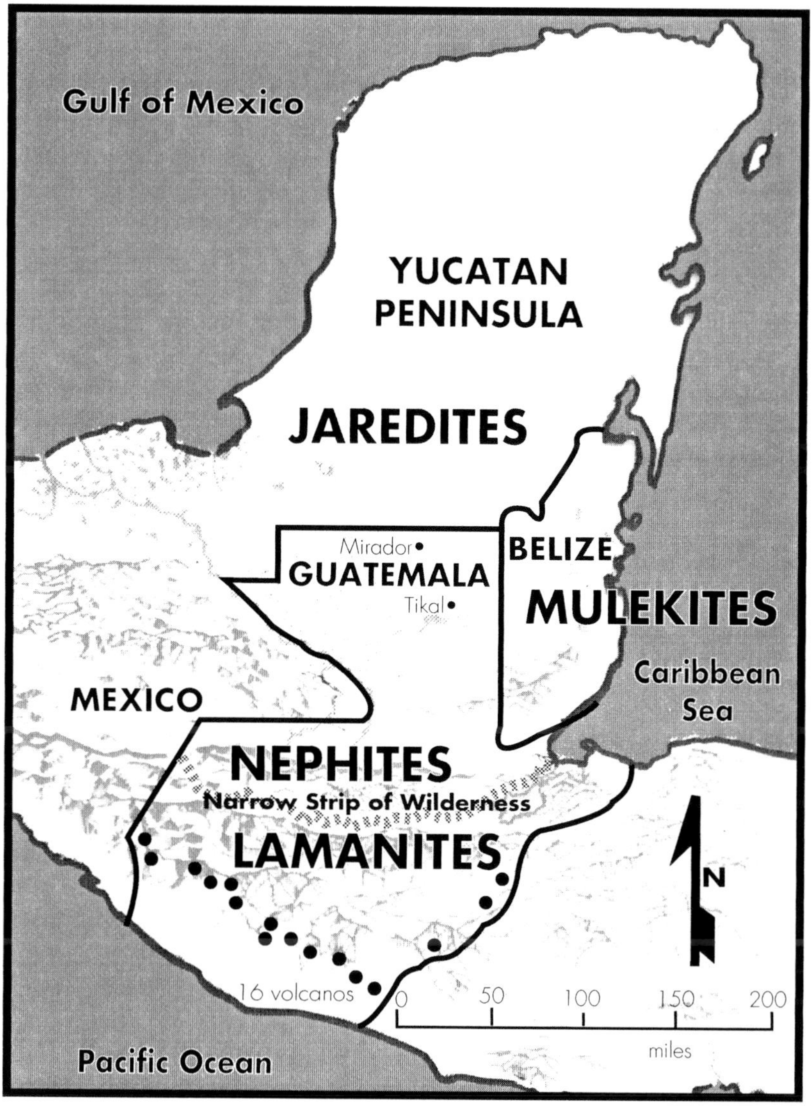

Narrow Strip of Wilderness at the junction of two massive tektonic plates of earth where over-thrusting and lateral movement caused massive earthquakes.

north plate (mass of earth) appears from geologic maps to have also moved south over the south plate. Such movement would account for the earth to be "carried up upon the city of Moronihah, that in the place of the city there became a great mountain." (3 Nephi 8:10.) Scriptures indicate that Moronihah was probably near where over-thrusting occurred, and near the land of the Lamanites (Alma 63:15), and that the city became very corrupt and was destroyed. (3 Nephi 8:25.)

A narrow strip of wilderness exists along the massive fault at the junction of the two plates which later in Nephite history divided the Lamanites on the south from the Nephites living in the land of Zarahemla on the north. (Alma 22:7.) The fault at the junction of the two tectonic plates, as well as the narrow strip of wilderness, existed before the crucifixion, but the massive over-thrusting that occurred when Christ was crucified caused more extensive damage. Today few roads exist across this narrow strip of wilderness.

When one mass of earth (a tectonic plate) moves over another, not only is a mountain created but also tension cracks develop behind the over-thrusting plate and the earth is pulled apart. Three distinct major faults exist north of the narrow strip of wilderness in Guatemala. In all three abnormalities, the faults and fracture zones are oriented east-west, parallel to the junction of the two tectonic plates and the narrow strip of wilderness.

Sunken Valley

Major east-west faults are on the north and south sides of a sunken valley which is near the east end and north of the narrow strip of wilderness. (Figure 4.) The earth dropped down when the land on each side had been pulled apart. This geologic condition was caused by the over-thrusting of the north tectonic plate which created the narrow strip of wilderness. The sunken valley is now mostly covered with waters of Lago de Izabal and El Golfete. One wonders if the name of the lagoon Izabal has any historical tie to the account in Alma 39:3 of the harlot Isabel. She was in this general area according to the scriptures.

figure 4

A sunken valley now covered with water which is near the east end and north of the Narrow Strip of Wilderness at the junction of two tectonic plates.

An example of a sunken valley is the Salt Lake Valley in Utah where anciently the valley floor dropped 5000 feet when over-thrusting occurred. Over the centuries, the valley has been mostly filled with sediment from the adjacent mountains.

The city of Moroni is recorded in the book to be near the east sea and north of the narrow strip of wilderness. (Alma 62:25; 3 Nephi 8:9; 9:4.) The suggested location of the city is in the sunken valley inundated with water from the Caribbean Sea.

Line Bountiful

While in Guatemala recently, I obtained detailed geologic maps which show a prominent 60-mile long fault 15 miles south of Tikal in northern Guatemala. This extends east from the northwest side of lake Peten Itza near Flores. (Figure 5.) Another 20 miles of fault is inferred to the east. This major fault is likely the "Line Bountiful" referred to in Alma 22:32 as being in the vicinity of the narrow neck of land between the land northward and the land southward with a sea west and a sea east. Several references in the Book of Mormon refer to the land northward as being adjacent to the narrow pass or neck. The significance of the line Bountiful in identifying the Book of Mormon lands will be discussed in detail in Chapter 9.

figure 5

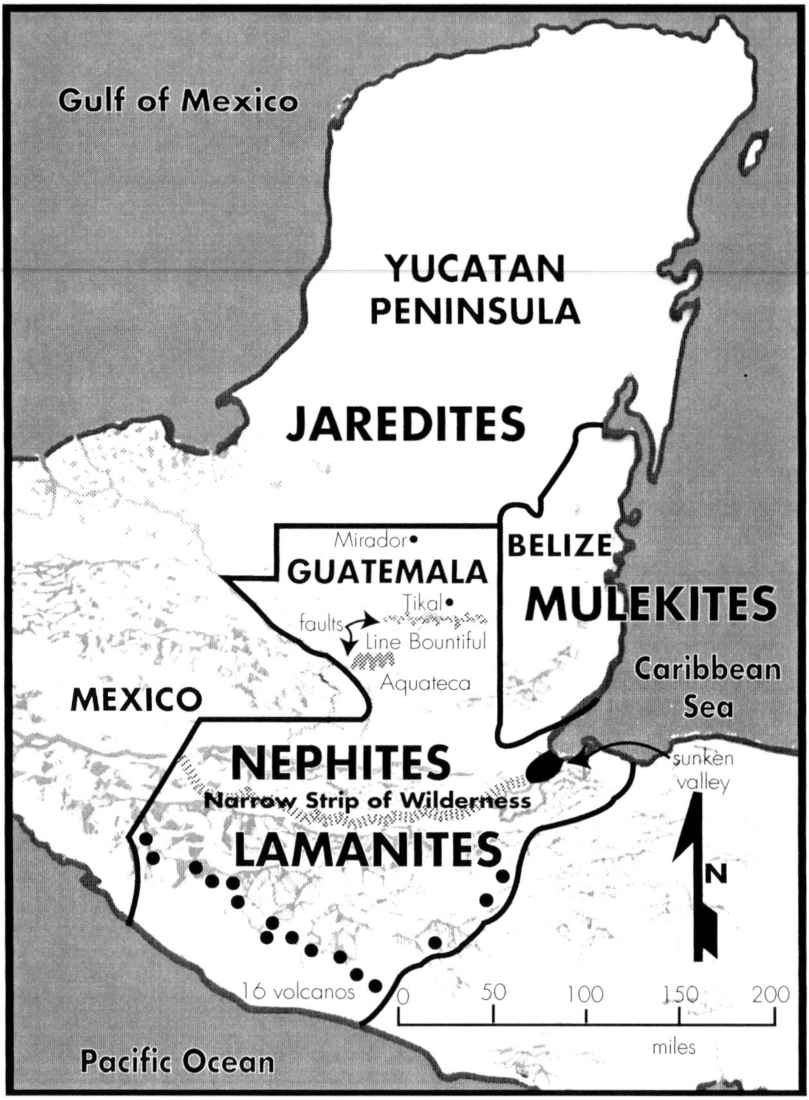

The Line Bountiful, a 60-mile long fault, and also a deep chasm at Aguateca in northern Guatemala.

Deep Chasm and an Escarpment

A major fault, a deep linear chasm several feet wide, exists in central Guatemala, about 100 miles north of the narrow strip of wilderness (see figure 5.) It is 70 miles southwest of Tikal at the ancient city of Aquatech. (National Geographic, Feb. 1993.)

Changing the Whole Face of the Land Northward

To "change the whole face," as recorded in 3 Nephi 8:11-12, probably means to alter the outline as well as the surface features within the land to the north. The massive movement of the North American Plate over and to the west along the south Caribbean Plate would result in an increase in elevation of the north plate. An increase in elevation of one or two hundred feet would certainly change the shoreline. Thus, today's shore line may be significantly different from the shoreline before the crucifixion.

Searchers for the narrow pass have suggested the Isthmus of Tehuantepec or the Panama Canal zone (see figure 1), but both have a sea north and sea south, not west and east as clearly stated in the Book of Mormon.

Figure 6 shows where it is believed "the whole face of the land northward" was changed in northern Guatemala, Belize and the Yucatan Peninsula. This suggested location for the narrow passage with seas west and east is very important, for it results in a harmony and consistency of all scriptures pertaining to Book of Mormon lands.

figure 6

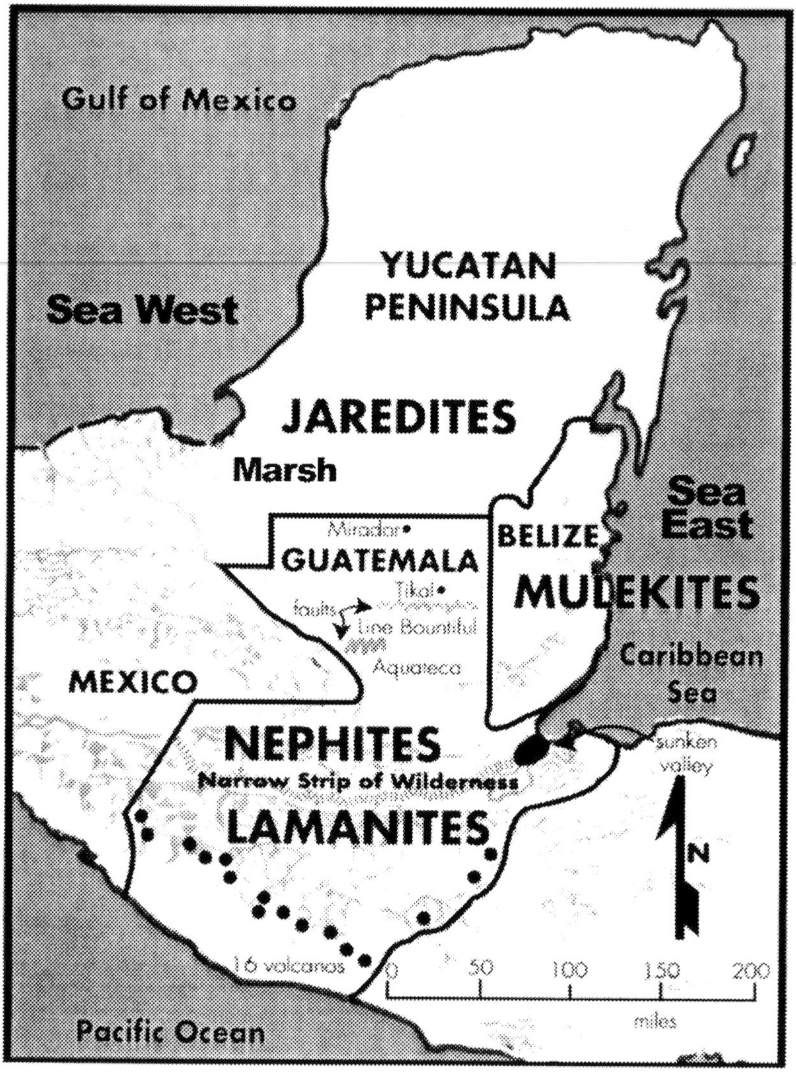

Seas west and east of the Narrow Pass before the crucifixion.

Seas West and East from the Narrow Pass

The narrow pass, or neck, or passage is a very significant physical feature in the Book of Mormon. It divided the land of Zarahemla from the land northward. "And now, it was only a distance of a day and a half's journey for a Nephite, on the line Bountiful and the land Desolation, from the east to the west sea;...there being a small neck of land between the land northward and the land southward." (Alma 22:32.) Several passages of scripture refer to the narrow pass having a sea on west and on the east. And Hagoth launched his ships into "the west sea, by the narrow neck which led into the land northward." (Alma 69:5.)

After the crucifixion, the elevation of the land northward was elevated by over-thrusting the land southward. Much of the land under the seas west and east of the narrow pass became marshy areas with numerous small tributaries. (See figure 7.)

Several ancient cities have been discovered within the approximate east sea area shown in figure 7. Archaeologists have identified several as having been occupied sometime during Nephite times. One ancient city, Lamanai, was occupied continuously from 500 B.C. to the 9th century A.D. Continuing research may identify other cities occupied before the crucifixion at A.D. 33. Islands and promontories undoubtedly existed adjacent to and within the general area of the east sea. Recent topographic maps show numerous rivers, tributaries, and marshes east of the narrow pass.

figure 7

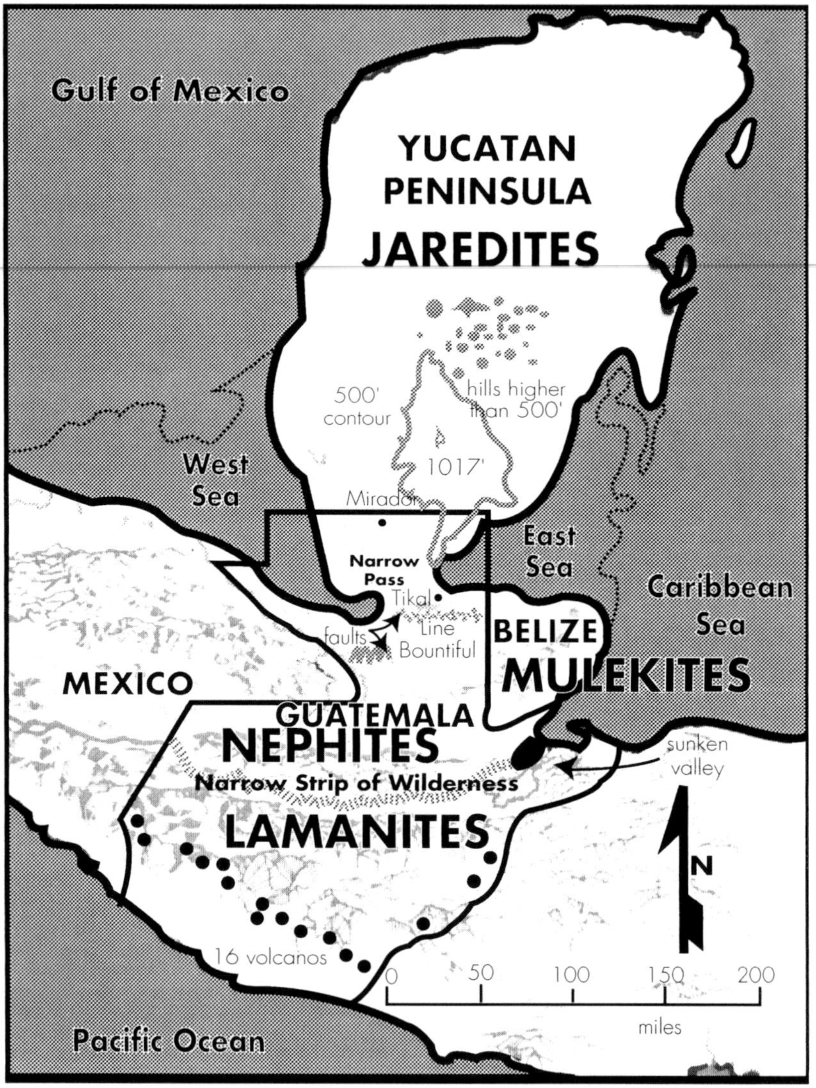

Higher ground and hills north of the Narrow Pass.

Within the proposed west sea area, only a few ancient cities have been discovered. The west sea was a more prominent and deeper sea, for in 55 B.C. Hagoth launched "an exceedingly large ship...into the west sea, by the narrow neck which led into the land northward." (Alma 63:5.) Recent maps of the area west of the narrow pass show more marsh land and poorer drainage patterns than the area east of the pass. Much of the land west is still not occupied.

Higher Ground and Hills

North of the narrow pass is higher ground and numerous hills. (Figure 7.) The Jaredite hill Ramah which was the Nephite hill Cumorah could have been one of these hills. Subsequent discussion of the Jaredite and Nephite scripture will discuss this possibility.

Summary

The changes in the land which occurred at the time of the crucifixion were great, especially in the land northward where the face of the whole land changed. Within the country of Guatemala, physical features exist which clearly explain the devastation that occurred including cities that were burned, or buried, or sunk into the sea. A narrow strip of wilderness exists along the junction of two massive tectonic plates of earth causing land to sink and creating extensive fractures in the earth. To the north a long fault could be the "Line Bountiful." North of the Line Bountiful a narrow pass was very likely bounded by a sea on the west and by a sea on the east. Today that narrow pass containing the major ancient cities of Tikal and

Mirador are a corridor for north-south travel with marshy areas and numerous tributaries to the west and to the east. To the north of the narrow pass, higher ground and numerous hills could have been the location of the Jaredite hill Ramah and the Nephite hill Cumorah. Many ancient cities were built north of the narrow pass.

Geologic, topographic, and archaeological evidence support the suggestion that Guatemala, Belize and the Yucatan Peninsula were lands of the Book of Mormon. The summary of physical clues in this chapter will be followed by a detailed discussion of the scriptural record of these people. Chapter 9 is a more detailed discussion of the narrow pass, Bountiful, Hagoth, and Cumorah. The overview that has been presented in this chapter should help the reader better follow the more detailed presentation which follows.

Sequence of Presentation

The Book of Mormon presents first the account of the Nephites, then the Mulekites, and finally the account of the Jaredites. Proceeding with the search for the home lands of these three groups, the search will be enhanced by reversing the sequence, by first discussing the Jaredites, then the Mulekites, and finally the Nephites. The land of the Book of Mormon is more easily understood by having the Jaredite and Mulekite records in focus before discussing the more detailed record of the Nephites.

4

The Jaredites

Jaredite Migrations to the Ocean

The Jaredite record in the Book of Ether begins near the land of the Tower of Babel. The Tigris and Euphrates valley, now the land of Iraq, is considered to be the site of the Tower. Great wickedness existed among the people under the leadership of Nimrod. The people of the Tower were attempting to reach heaven by physically building a stairway upward. (Genesis 11:4.)

The Lord decreed that the people's Adamic language would be confounded. (Genesis 11:6-7.) A dispersion of the people commenced.

A righteous group under the leadership of Jared was living apart from the less righteous people who were building the Tower. Jared's people were striving to get to heaven by living the commandments of God given to them by their righteous fathers.

Jared requested that his brother, who was "highly favored of the Lord," pray to God requesting that their language not be confounded. His prayer was answered. (Ether 1:34-35.)

Their initial travel to "a land which is choice above all other lands" was "down into the valley [of Nimrod] which is northward." (Ether 1:42; 2:4.) This righteous branch was subsequently led by divine providence to a "chosen land." After the Jaredites went northward from their homeland to the valley of Nimrod and then into the wilderness, the direction of migration is assumed here to be westward, not eastward as some writers have suggested.

A clue to their travel west is in Ether 2:5. The Lord commanded them "that they go forth into the wilderness, yea, into that quarter where there never had man been." Jaredite travel occurred shortly after the dispersion from the Tower commenced. Archaeological and historical evidence confirm that a significant civilization developed early in southeast China, but not until later in southern Europe. (I have seen the evidence in China.) Also travel eastward across the Tian Shan Mountains, then north of the Himalaya Mountains and Tibet, and across the Gobi Desert would have been very difficult and much harder than across southern Europe.

The Jaredites are recorded to have built barges to cross many waters (Ether 2:6), perhaps the Black Sea. This assumed migration westward could have been across the plains of southwestern Russia, up the Danube River valley, and north of the Alps and Pyrenees Mountains. This route would have been relatively easy, much easier than toward the east.

Figure 8 shows the assumed route of the Jaredites from the vicinity of Mount Ararat into the valley of Nimrod, then northward and westward across what we know now as southwestern Asia and central Europe.

figure 8

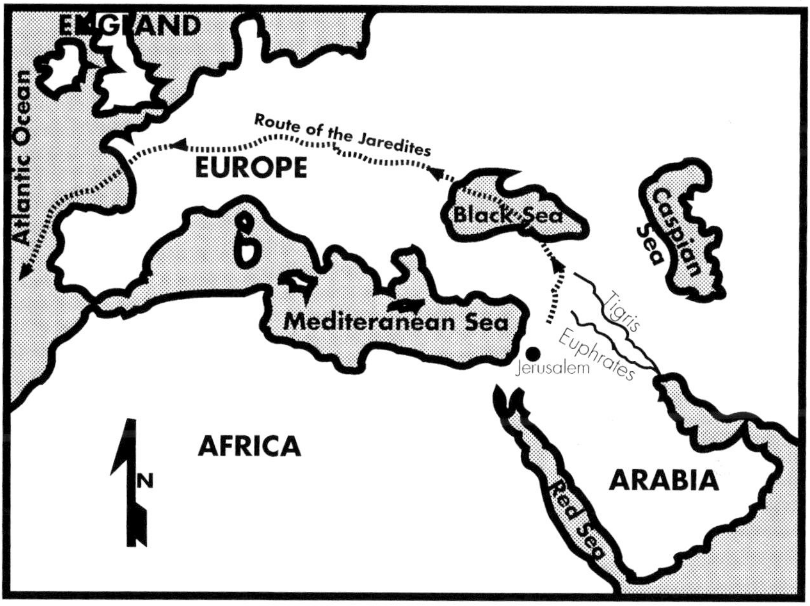

Migration of the Jaredites from south of Mount Ararat to the west coast of Europe.

The Pyrenees Mountains between France and Spain contain peaks above 11,000 feet with areas of permanent snow. Perhaps the brother of Jared went to the Pyrenees when he "went forth unto the mount Shelem, because of its exceeding height, and did molten out of a rock sixteen small stones. "The Lord touched the stones, and they gave light to the barges built to cross the sea. (Ether 3:1,4,6.)

Another reason for suggesting that they may have traveled westward lies in the legends and early recorded history of the Welsh and Irish. They claim to have descended from Gomer, the firstborn son of Japheth. Gomer apparently came to the British Isles about the same time the Jaredites were migrating from the Tower, and the earliest construction at Stonehenge was about 2300 B.C. (Hansen, *Whence Came They*, page 29.) Perhaps some of the friends of Jared and his brother went to Great Britain. Pursuing this clue will shed light upon the Jaredites and their possible lineage to Japheth.

Recall that Noah had three sons—Japheth, Shem and Ham. Some of the descendants of Ham and his wife Egyptus went to Egypt and became the Pharaohs. (Abraham 1:23-24.) Abraham, from the lineage of Shem, was living in the land of his fathers, in the land of Ur, of the Chaldees, in the Tigris or Euphrates valley. (Abraham 2:3-4.)

Thus, we can reasonably assume that descendants of Noah dispersed from the vicinity of Mount Ararat, with Ham going southwest, Shem toward the west, and Japheth to the north. The Bible Dictionary (page 710 in the L.D.S. edition of the scriptures) states that Japheth's "descendants were dispersed over the European coasts of the Mediterranean and the districts adjoining the Black and Caspian seas." In Malta, France, Wales and Ireland similar mounds and burials have been found dating from about 2500 B.C. The dominant carving on these edifices is the sacred scroll, indicating these people had a common origin.

Josephus (chapter 6, pages 30-31) states that the sons of Japheth (spelled Japhet in *The Complete Works of Josephus*) settled themselves "upon lands...which none had inhabited before." And as quoted earlier, Ether 2:5 states that the Jaredites also went "into the wilderness, yea, into that quarter where there never had man been." Were Jaredites also from Japheth? Did some of the friends of Jared and his brother go to Great Britain where Welch legends and records state that they are from the lineage of Gomer, the firstborn son Japheth? Jared, his brother, and their friends were a blessed people who were provided very sacred spiritual guidance to a land choice above all other lands.

On the shore of the "great body of water" the Jaredites were commanded to build barges like those they had built earlier in their journey. The barges were small, light upon the water, and built watertight both top and bottom like a dish. The ends were peaked, and the barges were the length of a tree. An opening in the top could be secured shut so that no water would enter, but it could be opened when fresh air was needed. (Ether 2:16-17, 20.) The eight barges undoubtedly had no sails or ability to steer for they were closed and at times were buried in the sea. They were to be carried by ocean currents to the "promised land."

The remarkable account of the Brother of Jared making 16 clear stones is well known. The Lord touched these stones causing them to give light so the inside of the eight barges would not be dark. (Ether 3:1-6,13.) The appearance of the Lord Jehovah to the Brother of Jared was a sacred event, providing a spiritual foundation for this chosen branch of Noah's posterity. Likewise, Lehi and

Joseph Smith were given sacred knowledge as a foundation for their prophetic ministries.

The eight unique barges were cast into the sea, and for 344 days (nearly a year) they were buffeted by wind and waves as they crossed the great water. (Ether 6:4-11.)

The route across the sea is critical to locating the land of the Jaredites in America. To know whether they crossed the Pacific Ocean and landed on the west coast near the Isthmus of Tehuantepec where the ancient Olmecs lived, or whether they crossed the Atlantic Ocean and landed on the Yucatan Peninsula and were separated from the Olmecs is critical. (See figure 1.)

Jaredites Crossing the Ocean

Some authors have assumed that the Jaredites traveled eastward across China and that their barges were carried across the Pacific Ocean to the western coast of lower Mexico near the Isthmus of Tehuantepec.

Barges cast into the China Sea would have been carried by clockwise currents into the north Pacific Ocean. There they would have encountered some winter weather and extremely cold water temperatures. They had no heat (fire) in their barges. (Ether 2:23.) Many times they were "buried in the depths of the sea." (Ether 2:24; 6:6.) Water temperatures of the north Pacific Ocean are so cold that the Jaredites would not likely have survived in unheated barges. Winter air temperatures would have been colder than the average water temperatures of 40-50 degrees Fahrenheit. (Weigel, Oceanographical Engineering, page 385.)

On the other hand, if the Jaredite barges were cast adrift from the western shores of Europe, they would have been carried by clockwise ocean currents across the mid Atlantic Ocean in waters of moderate temperature. The severe winds mentioned would have blown the barges, with their "upturned ends," from the local clockwise currents off the west coast of Europe into the main Atlantic current, then southward toward the equator, and then westward into the clockwise Caribbean current. (Figure 9.) Thus, Jaredites would have landed on the east coast of the Americas, not on the west coast as some authors have assumed.

figure 9

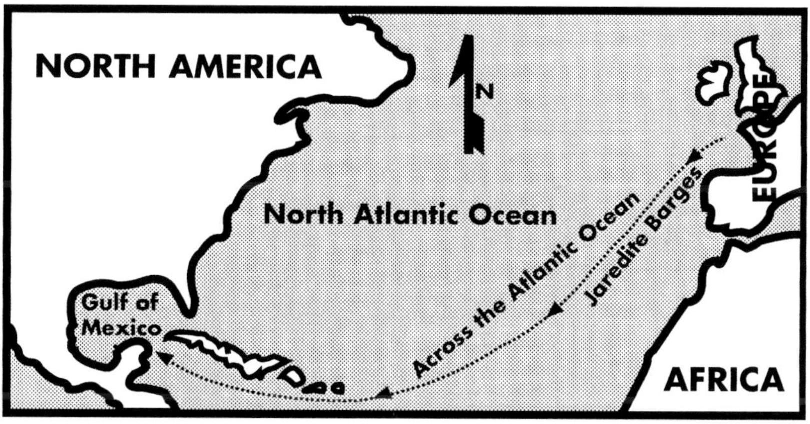

Jaredite barges carried by ocean currents across the Atlantic Ocean from Europe to America.

Where the Jaredites Landed

The Book of Ether does not contain sufficient detail to identify specifically where the Jaredites landed.

However, when Ether's record is considered along with the brief record of the Mulekites and the detailed account of the Nephites, the probable location of the land of the Jaredites can be reasonably assumed. One example of this correlation is that the land of the Jaredites is north of the land of the Nephites. (Ether 7:6, 15:1; Alma 22:30.)

Thus, based upon the overall account in the Book of Mormon, to be discussed in subsequent chapters, the assumption has been made here that the "land of their [the Jaredite's] first inheritance" (Ether 7:16-17) was on the Yucatan Peninsula in Eastern Mexico. (Figure 10.)

The Olmec Theory

Some writers have suggested that the Jaredites were the ancient Olmecs who lived on the Isthmus of Tehuantepec in Mexico, west of the Yucatan. (Figure 10.) If Olmecs were Jaredites, then the Jaredite land would have been in the Isthmus, not to the east on the Yucatan Peninsula.

Archaeological studies have now given a relatively clear understanding of the ancient Olmecs. Several recent publications and recently discovered maps and investigations confirm that the Chinese were traveling and establishing communities along the western coast of North America in Jaredite times. (*Archaeology*, March/April 1996, page 58; *Time*, July 1, 1996, page 56.)

figure 10

Land of the Jaredites on the Yucatan Peninsula in eastern Mexico.

Huge 10-foot carved-basalt Olmec heads have been unearthed in the Isthmus of Tehuantepec near the Tuxtla Mountains in Mexico. (Figure 11.) The massive carved heads showing Oriental characteristics were often marred and completely buried by another group of ancient people in an apparent effort to eradicate the history of the Olmec.

figure 11

Huge 10-foot carved-bassalt Olmec head unearthed in the Isthmes of tehuantepec in Mexico.

figure 12

Chinese Terracotta warrior buried about 225 B.C. near the tomb of Qin Shi Huang di (*Curtural Atlas of China*, p. 8).

Note the oriental similarity between figure 11 of the Olmec head and figure 12 showing the head of a life size terra cotta warrior "excavated near the tomb of Qin Shi Huang di [about 225 B.C.]." (*Cultural Atlas of China*, page 8.) The resemblance of facial characteristics and the outline of the head covering which is likely a helmet, is startling.

An authority on Olmecs, archaeologist Dr. Ann Cypers, recently gave a lecture at Brigham Young University. She had spent several years in Mexico excavating Olmec ruins. Dr. Cypers said that Olmecs were likely Oriental, were not very large but were quite muscular, and that the helmets on the colossal heads indicated rulership.

These statements by Dr. Cypers support my assumptions concerning the Olmecs. Especially significant is her statement, based upon recently discovered burials, that Olmecs were not very large. Recall from Mosiah 8:7-10 that Limhi sent 43 of his people from the city of Nephi to find the land of Zarahemla. This party did not find Zarahemla, but did discover a land that had been occupied by a numerous people. The expedition also found the Jaredite record written by Ether, and also brought back breastplates which were large. This indicates that the Jaredites were large, not short as were the Olmecs. Thus, Dr. Cypers statement about the Olmecs is further evidence that the Olmecs were not Jaredites.

The following is taken from a recent informative summary of the Olmecs published in *Time*, July 1, 1996, pages 56-58: most of the Olmec habitations were near the Isthmus of Tehuantepec in Mexico, they were from Asia, the "Olmec society was in full flow by 1200 B.C." along the north shore of the Isthmus. A great pyramid was built to the east at La Venta around 800 B.C. Seventeen stone heads ranging in height from 5 feet to 11 feet are presumed to have been carved between 1200 B.C. to 900 B.C. Olmec art consisting of images of "dragons, birds, dwarfs, hunchbacks and, most important, the were-jaguar (part human, part jaguar)—indicates a belief in the super natural and in shamanism. Olmec-style human figures typically have squarish facial features with full lips, a flat nose, pronounced jowls and slanting eyes." Child sacrifice occurred. About 300 B.C., Olmec civilization vanished.

Does this sound like a Jaredite civilization, worthy of having its record included in the Book of Mormon? Olmecs were not Jaredites.

Jaredite Leadership

A possible clue to the relationship between the Olmecs and the Jaredites can be gleaned from a close look at the list of Jaredite leaders recorded in Ether 1:7-32. The time from the first leader, Jared, to the last leader, Coriantumer, is approximately 2500 years, an average of 75 years per leader. (The Bible confirms that earlier leaders would have lived longer than later leaders.) Ether recorded the name and the righteousness of each leader, except for a conquering people who held six consecutive legitimate Jaredite leaders in captivity (leader number 18, Hearthan, to leader number 23, Com.) This period of continuous captivity may have lasted as long as 300 years, assuming 50 years per leader. This captivity is estimated to have lasted from 800 B.C. to 500 B.C. The footnote at the bottom of this page details the basis for these assumed dates.

Some Jaredite leaders before and after this continuous period of captivity were also in captivity or were overthrown, but in these times the new leader and the deposed leader were usually named and identified as Jaredites. During the time when six consecutive Jaredite leaders were in captivity, their captor was not identified. This suggests that the aggressor and his army were not Jaredites. Is it possible that the aggressors were Olmecs who lived to the west in the Isthmus of Tehuantepec? Olmec decline may have coincided with the end of the approximately 300 years of oppression of Jaredites by a people other then themselves, probably about 500 B.C. The Olmec culture flourished between 1200 and 400 B.C. (*National Geographic*, Nov. 1993, page 92.)

Other Clues to Jaredite Land

The Book of Mormon clearly states that the southern part of Jaredite land, called Desolation by the Nephites, was near the Nephite land of Bountiful, and that Desolation was near but north of the narrow pass. (Alma 22:31-33; 50:34; 52:9; 63:5.)

In Omni 1:5 a date of 279 B.C. was recorded by Amaron, then Chemish and Abinadom each add a verse. Finally Amaleki spoke of Mosiah finding the people of Zarahemla (Omni 1:12), between 279 and 130 B.C. Since the people of Zarahemla found Coriantumr, the last survivor of the Jaredite battle, it is assumed that the final battle occurred about 200 B.C. Ether records seven Jaredite leaders after the period of continuous captivity, a period of approximately 300 years. These estimated dates and periods would indicate that the time of Jaredite captivity extended from approximately 800 to 500 B.C.

The land of Bountiful was a wilderness "filled with all manner of wild animals of every kind, a part of which had come from the land northward for food." (Alma 22:31.) Because of drought conditions and the necessity to flee from poisonous serpents, the flocks of the Jaredites "began to flee... toward the land southward, which was called by the Nephites Zarahemla." (Ether 9:31.) Thus, the Jaredite land was northward from both the Nephite lands of Bountiful and Zarahemla.

A forest lay to the south of Jaredite land because the Jaredites "did go into the land southward, to hunt for food...for the land was covered with animals of the forest." (Ether 10:19.) Also "they built a great city by the narrow neck of land, by the place where the sea divides the land." (Ether 10:20.) Could either of the major ancient cities of Tikal or Mirador be the great city built by the Jaredites? (See figure 10.)

The records just cited place the southern boundary of Jaredite territory near the narrow neck of land, and north of the Nephite Bountiful. The Book of Mormon indicates that seas are also near the narrow neck of land, a sea to the west and a sea to the east (Alma 50:34; Mormon 4:3), and a seashore is not far from the land of Moron. (Ether 14:13.) Moron was on higher ground, because an army had to "come up" to attack the land of Moron. (Ether 7:5.) Perhaps the land of Moron was on the higher ground north of the narrow pass. (See figure 7.)

The waters of Ripliancum, meaning large—to exceed all—lie toward the north for Shiz fled southward from the waters of Ripliancum. (Ether 15:8-10.) In chapter 9, the narrow neck of land and the seas to the west and to the east will be discussed in more detail.

The Jaredites did work in all manner of ore and "they did cast up mighty heaps of earth to get ore." (Ether 10:23.) Thus, when identifying the land of the Jaredites, a region where evidence of past mining now exists, must be found in or near the Jaredite land. The Puuc hills in the northwest part of the Yucatan do contain minerals.

Within three generations of the landing of the Jaredites, the rebellious Corihor went over and dwelt in the land of Nehor. (Ether 7:4.) The mention of Nehor so early in Jaredite times confirms that this group of Antichrists was an adverse influence which continued down into Nephite history where evil men named Nehor were present. Their influence is always located on the borders of the land away from where the more righteous Jaredites and Nephites lived.

Final Jaredite Battles

The battles that occurred during the final Jaredite years were described by Ether in some detail. The sequence and relative locations of these battles are shown in figure 13. Scriptural references are given for each location, and the proximity to seas are noted twice. Direction is recorded only three times: (1) eastward from the plains of Agosh to the borders by the seashore (Ether 14:15, 26), (2) when Shiz went southward from the waters of Ripliancum to Ogath where he prepared for the final battle (Ether 15:8,10), and (3) when King Omer fled supposedly from Moron, and traveled many days, passed the hill

figure 13

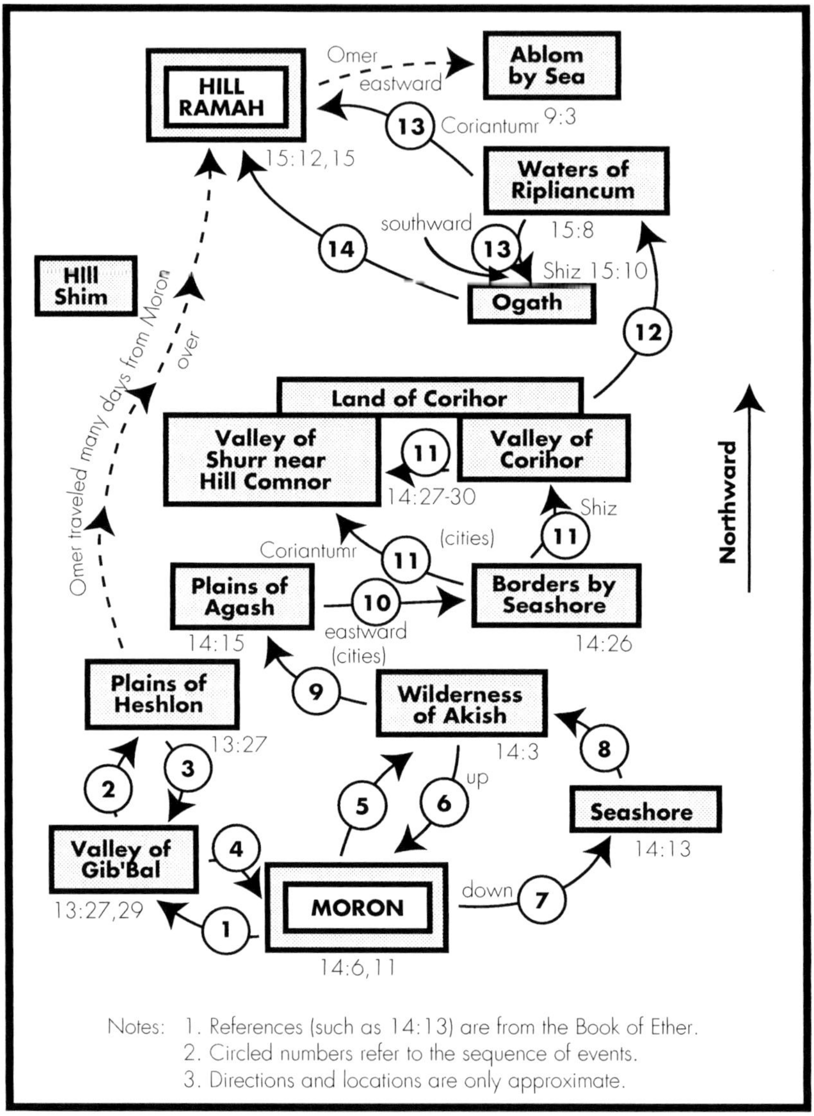

Final Jaredite battles and Omer's flight from Moron.

Shem and later the hill Ramah, and went eastward to Ablom by the sea. (Ether 9:3.) Moroni states that the Jaredite Hill Ramah is the Nephite Cumorah. (Ether 15:11.)

Limited as the clues are to Jaredite lands and travel, these clues nevertheless are useful when combined with clues from Mulekite and Nephite records presented in later chapters.

5

Land of Mulek and Zarahemla

Mulek and the People of Zarahemla

Knowledge of Mulek and the people of Zarahemla is fragmentary. The Bible states that Zedekiah, king of the Kingdom of Judah, was carried captive into Babylon, and his sons were slain. (2 Kings 25:7.) But the Book of Mormon records that a son of Zedekiah named Mulek survived, and that he and his companions were "brought by the Lord across the great waters, into the land where Mosiah discovered them; and they had dwelt there from that time forth." (Omni 1:16.) "Now the land south was called Lehi, and the land north was called Mulek, which was after the sons of Zedekiah; for the Lord did bring Mulek into the land north, and Lehi into the land south." (Helaman 6:10.)

"And at the time Mosiah discovered them, they [the people of Zarahemla] had become exceedingly numerous.

Nevertheless, they had had many wars and serious contentions, and had fallen by the sword from time to time; and their language had become corrupted; and they had brought no records with them; and they denied the being of their Creator; and Mosiah, nor the people of Mosiah, could understand them." (Omni 1:17.) The people of Zarahemla, discovered by Mosiah, were descendants "of Mulek, and those who came with him into the wilderness." (Mosiah 25:2.)

Several significant observations can be drawn from the above account of the Mulekites. First, Mulek's people were "brought by the Lord," a righteous branch of the tribe of Judah. Second, Mulek and his people were brought to the land of the north, but the record speaks of Zarahemla and his people, not Mulek, coming up into the wilderness. They established the city of Zarahemla approximately 200 B.C., (400 years after Mulek fled from Jerusalem about 586 B.C.) It seems that Zarahemla had led the more righteous Mulekites up into the wilderness to a place of refuge away from the place of their first landing where they had numerous wars and contentions. In somewhat the same manner Mosiah led the more righteous Nephites away and down from the city of Nephi.

Mulek's people who were led away by Zarahemla were known as the people of Zarahemla, and Lehi's people led away by Mosiah were known as the people of Mosiah. Mosiah was a righteous Nephite prophet, and he taught the people of Zarahemla his language and became their king. The people of Zarahemla were teachable and willing to follow Mosiah's prophetic leadership. Both groups were select and choice people.

Significance of the Name Zarahemla

The identity of the people of Mulek may be in the name "Zarahemla," and may provide a clue to why Mulek, a son of Zedekiah, was not captured and slain as were his brothers. (2 Kings 25:7.)

Judah, one of the twelve sons of Jacob (Israel), had twin sons, Pharez and Zarah. Pharez, the first born, became the ancestor of Solomon, David, and Jesus. Many descendants of Zarah, however, left the camp of Israel after they had fled from Egypt and were in the wilderness. (Hansen, *Whence Came They*, pages 37-38.)

The name "Zara-hemla" suggests that Mulek's mother was from the branch of Zarah of the tribe of Judah. This fact could account for the Biblical statement that the sons of king Zedekiah were killed, that his sons were from the royal branch of Pharez. Mulek survived apparently because his mother, another wife of king Zedekiah—was not of the royal line, but was a descendant of Zarah. She had fled with Mulek, who undoubtedly was an infant son or perhaps had not been born yet, and was not captured by the invading Babylonians.

Loss of Language and Religion

The approximately 400 years from the time Mulek fled from Jerusalem until Mosiah arrived at the city of Zarahemla provided ample opportunity for the Mulekites to lose their language, since they brought no records with them. Furthermore, at their place of first landing, they may have had contact with Jaredites who spoke a different language for we know that Coriantumr, the sole survivor of the Jaredite battle at the hill Ramah spent the final "nine moons" of his life with the people of Zarahemla and was buried by them. (Omni 1:21.)

Jaredite names are prevalent in Mulekite and Nephite history, names such as Coriantumr, Nehor, Kishkumen, Shim, and Morianton. There is nothing in the Book of Mormon that shows direct contact between the Nephites and the Jaredites.

Another possibility for the change of language may have been contact with Phoenicians. When the Babylonians attacked Jerusalem from the east, the family of Mulek would have fled to the west into the land of the Phoenicians or southward to Egypt where Phoenician ships were also present. By 600 B.C., Phoenicians were sailing throughout the Mediterranean Sea and beyond. Even as early as 900 B.C., Phoenicians were shipping tin from Cornwall in England, some of which was used in Solomon's Temple. (Hansen, *Whence Came They*, page 88.) Paul R. Cheesman in *World of the Book of Mormon* (1984, pp. 135-142) presents twelve archaeological findings inferring early Phoenician presence in the Western Hemisphere. Also, Samuel D. Marble in *Before Columbus* (1980, pp. 31, 115, 138) indicates Phoenicians crossed the Atlantic as early as 1447 B.C., and about 500 B.C., 30,000 Phoenicians sailed past Gibraltar for the West.

Certainly as a son of royalty, Mulek and party had sufficient financial resources to purchase sea passage away from the land of Jerusalem, maybe even to America. Hence, prolonged association with Jaredites, and/or with Phoenicians, for 200 to 300 years would have resulted in a change in Mulekite language.

Land Where Mulekites Lived

From this somewhat fragmentary information and from the information contained in chapter 4 concerning the Jaredites, the land of the Mulekites can be approximated. (See figure 14.) The Jaredites, the Mulekites, and the Nephites (all three colonies) lived in the Yucatan or in Guatemala at the same time from about 600 B.C. to 400 B.C. and possibly as late as 200 B.C. As discussed in the previous chapter, the Jaredites were likely in the upper Yucatan north of the narrow pass. The Nephites were probably in Guatemala, as will be shown in the following chapter. About 200 B.C. under the leadership of Mosiah, the Nephites went north and found the people of Zarahemla. Descendants of Mulek had recently come up from their original home land in Belize and had built the city of Zarahemla. Their leader Zarahemla was still alive when Mosiah arrived.

The wilderness of Bountiful to the west of the land of Mulek would have isolated them from the Nephites to the southwest. The sea east of the narrow pass and north of the Mulekites would have isolated them from the main body of Jaredites to the northwest. Many ancient cities have been identified in Belize.

The land of Bountiful was probably northeast from Zarahemla near the narrow pass, and was not mentioned by Nephite prophets until after 90 B.C. Thus, the Nephites had probably not occupied Bountiful until at least 400 or 500 years after coming to America.

To avoid wars and contentions, Zarahemla undoubtedly lead the more righteous Mulekites away from the land of their first inheritance near the coast. They apparently traveled inland and built the city of Zarahemla. (Figure 14.)

figure 14

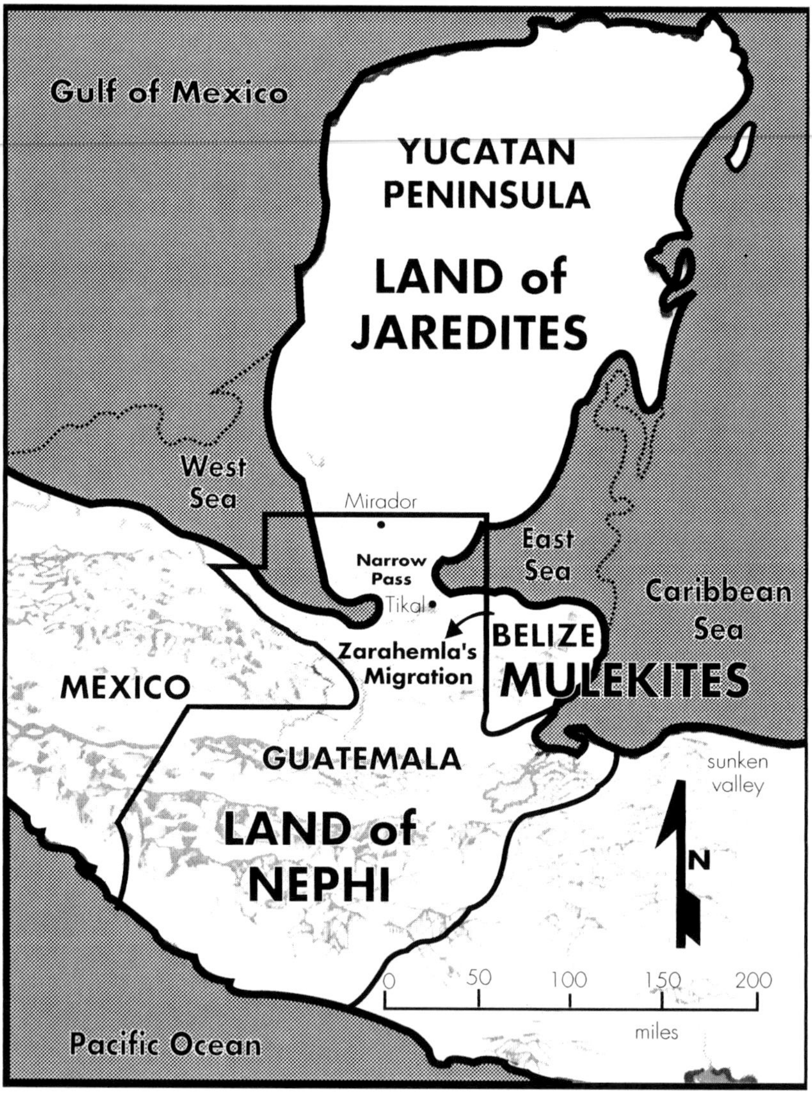

Migration of Zarahemla from the land of Mulek about 200 B.C.

6

Land of Nephi

Father Lehi

Father Lehi, from the lineage of Joseph thru his son Manasseh, was a prophet in Jerusalem about 600 B.C. He warned the people of the destruction that awaited them, if they did not repent. Jeremiah, from the lineage of Judah, was simultaneously prophesying destruction. Both Lehi and Jeremiah were rejected and threatened with death if they did not stop preaching. The Lord commanded Lehi to take his family and depart into the wilderness. (1 Nephi 2:1-2.) Apparently the danger was immediate for Lehi left his house, the land of this inheritance, and his gold, silver and precious things, taking only his family, provisions, and tents.

Lehi is thought to have been a wealthy man, a trader likely with Egypt, for he had provisions readily available that would sustain his family in the wilderness. Also, he and his family apparently knew the Egyptian language and their method of writing. The Brass Plates were written in Egyptian. (Mosiah 1:4.) Mormon's abridgement and Moroni's writings were in reformed Egyptian. (Mormon 9:32.)

Nephi speaks of his father's many visions, and he detailed the vision known as the "Tree of Life." Undoubtedly Lehi was a very choice prophet. Not only was he close to the Lord, but also he was chosen to become the progenitor of the prophet leaders who produced the records found in the Book of Mormon, a powerful second testament of Christ and the keystone of the restoration and gathering of Israel. Have you ever wondered by what authority Lehi directed his sons to return and obtain the Plates of Brass? (1 Nephi 3:4.) Yes, the Lord commanded him, but Lehi might also have been the principle High Priest for that portion of the tribe of Joseph living within the Jerusalem area. Laban, the keeper of the record, was also a descendant of Joseph. (1 Nephi 5:16.)

After obtaining the Brass Plates (about 600 B.C.), Lehi and his family accompanied by Ishmael and his family traveled in a south-southeast direction down the east coast of the Red Sea. (1 Nephi 2:5; 16:13-14.) Then changing to a nearly eastward direction, they eventually came to a place they called Bountiful. They had traveled for eight years in the wilderness. (Figure 15.) "And we did behold the sea which we did call Irreantum, which, being interpreted, is many waters." (1 Nephi 17:5; see also 1 Nephi 17:1-4.)

figure 15

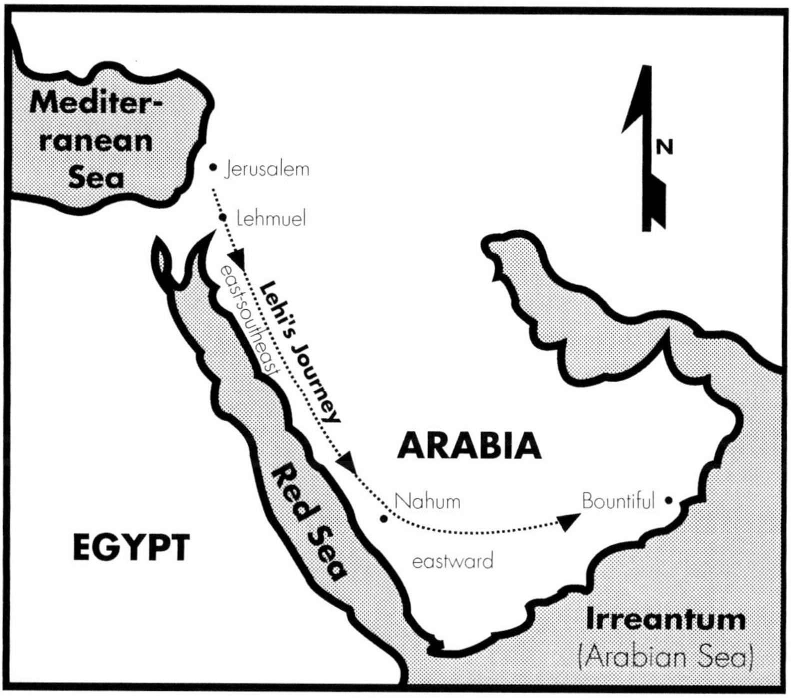

Lehi's journey from Jerusalem down the east side of the Red Sea to the Arabian Sea.

The Lord taught Lehi's son Nephi how to build a ship that would carry them across the sea. (1 Nephi 17:8.) This ship undoubtedly had sails for they "were driven forth before the wind towards the promised land." (1 Nephi 18:8.) The ship could be steered for the Lord had provided the Liahona (a compass) to point the way they should go. (1 Nephi 18:12,22.) When they lacked the required faith, the Liahona did not function, and they became lost and had great trouble. From their place of launching, trade winds would have carried them in a generally eastward direction across the Indian and Pacific oceans to the western shores of Central America..

A few authors have suggested that they sailed westward around Africa, across the Atlantic Ocean, and landed on the east coast of North America. But the general consensus today is that they came across the Pacific Ocean and landed in Southern Mexico or Guatemala. The early Nephite record places them in the western part of "the land of Nephi."

Lehi's Place of Landing

The place of landing was called the promised land. They pitched their tents, tilled the earth, and planted all their seeds which grew exceedingly. As they went into the wilderness, they found beasts of every kind, including the cow, the ox, the ass, the horse, the wild goat, and all manner of wild animals. And they found an abundance of ore, both of gold, and of silver, and of copper. (1 Nephi 18:23-25.) Information obtained recently while in Guatemala confirms that ore was available on the flanks of the nearby volcanoes and in the streams. Also rich deposits of ore were in the hills north of the faults near the present city of Hueheutenango in west central Guatemala. This was a choice land, a promised land.

Thus, the place of Lehi's landing was a fertile land with a favorable climate to grow the seeds they brought with them. And the adjacent wilderness contained a variety of precious metals. Both facts are important when attempting to identify their place of landing. The Pacific coast of Southern Mexico and Guatemala meets these criteria. (Figure 16.)

figure 16

Lehi crossed the Pacific Ocean and landed on the west coast of Mesoamerica.

Not long after landing, father Lehi prophesied, blessed his children, and then died. His sons Laman and Lemuel, and also the sons of Ishmael, became very rebellious and sought to take away Nephi's life. (2 Nephi 5:1-2.) The Lord warned Nephi and directed him to flee into the wilderness with the righteous segment of Lehi's family. Nephi took with him the Liahona, the sword of Laban, and the written records, including the Plates of Brass.

Nephi's City

After traveling many days in the wilderness, Nephi and his followers settled in an area which the people named Nephi. (2 Nephi 5:7-8.) Figure 17 shows the suggested general location for the city of Nephi in Guatemala where a relatively broad and very fertile area produces a variety of crops and sustains a sizeable native population. The round dots on figure 17 are the locations of 15 ancient cities built during Nephite times. They were built both west and east of the present sizeable city of Chimaltenango which is about 65 miles west from Guatemala city.

figure 17

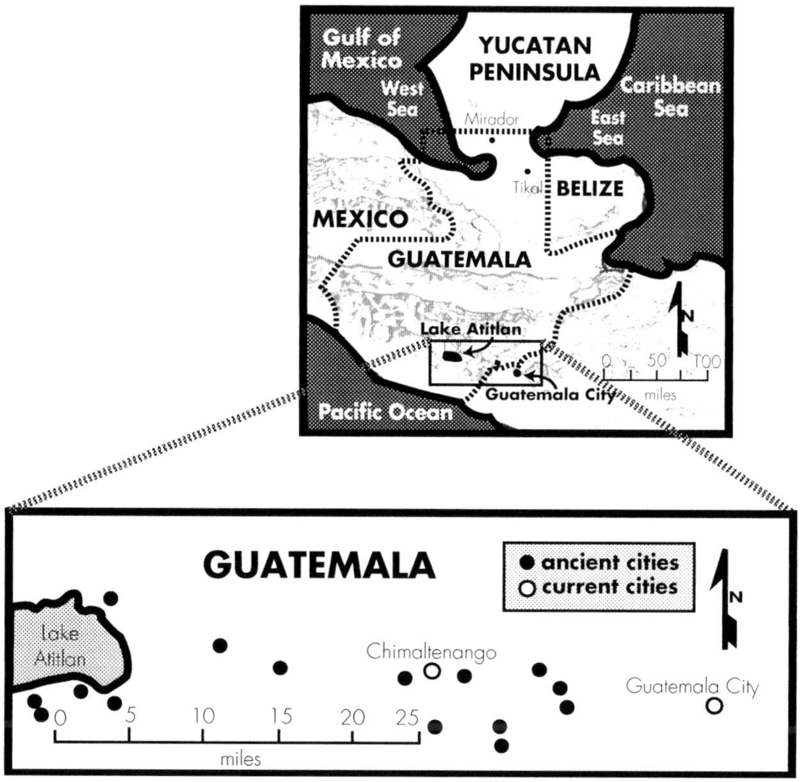

Suggested general location of the city and land of Nephi in Guatemala. The dots show where 15 ancient cities were built in Nephite times *(Mapa Arqueolocico de la Republica de Guatemala*, 1991).

The Book of Mormon describes many distinctive features of this chosen land which must be remembered when determining which one, if any, of the ancient sites shown in figure 17 was the city of Nephi.

1. This was a fertile area where their seeds grew well, and they reaped in abundance. Flocks,

herds, and animals of every kind were raised, and they did prosper. (1 Nephi 5:11.) Only at Nephi is wheat mentioned. (Mosiah 9:9.) Today, wheat is grown only in a limited area in the southwestern highlands of Guatemala. Thus, this place called Nephi was very fertile with a favorable climate, capable of supporting a growing and prosperous population for about 300 years (until the time when Mosiah lead the more righteous Nephites out of Nephi.) The land of Nephi was not a small valley.

2. Iron, copper, gold, silver, and other precious ores were in great abundance. (2 Nephi 5:15.)

3. Travel to Nephi was always "up" from any other city mentioned in the Book of Mormon. Nephi was on higher ground. (Omni 1:27; Mosiah 7:1; 10:1,6; Alma 22:3.)

4. A wilderness was north of Nephi, between Nephi and Zarahemla. (Alma 16:6-7; 31:3; 50:7.) Alma 22:27 states that a narrow strip of wilderness divided the land of Nephi from the land of Zarahemla.

5. The land of Nephi was toward the west, and along with their landing site was considered by the Nephites as the "land of our fathers' first inheritance." (Mosiah 9:1; 10:13; Alma 22:28; 54:12-13.)

6. At or near the city Nephi, the following existed:

   a. Nephi built a temple "after the manner of the temple of Solomon." (2 Nephi 5:16.)

b. The wicked Noah built a tower near the temple. (Mosiah 19:5.)

c. A hill and tower were north of the land of Shilom (Mosiah 7:5; 11:13), and "Ammon and three of his brethren...went down [from the hill] into the land of Nephi." (Mosiah 7:6.)

d. The Lamanite land of Shemlon could be seen from the tower near the temple. (Mosiah 19:6.)

e. Fields for crop production and grazing as well as a stream or spring "were away on the south of the land of Shilom" (Mosiah 9:14), and when Nephites in the field were attacked, they fled to the city of Nephi. (Mosiah 9:15.)

f. Nephi had walls, a gate and a "back pass, through the back wall, on the back side of the city" of Nephi. (Mosiah 7:10; 22:6.)

g. A secret pass existed "on the left of their [the Lamanites] camp." (Mosiah 22:7.)

h. The time required for Alma and his converts to travel from the waters of Mormon, not far from the city of Nephi, to Zarahemla was 22 days. (Mosiah 23:3; 24:25.)

The ancient city of Kaminal Juyu near Guatemala City has been suggested by some to be the city of Nephi. However, topographic conditions at Kaminal Juyu do not fit the book's description of Nephi and its surroundings. Also, an archaeological museum in Guatemala City contains hundreds of figurines from Kaminal Juyu that are clearly pagan. Righteous followers of Christ have never in the history of the world created satanic figures and statuettes depicting themselves or their gods. Kaminal Juyu was not the location of the city of Nephi.

Other Lands and Cities Near the City of Nephi

Several lands and cities near Nephi are mentioned during the missionary labors to the Lamanites of the sons of Mosiah (Ammon, Aaron, Omner, and Himni). Lamanite converts came from places called Ishmael, Middoni, Nephi, Shilom, Shemlon, Lemuel, and Shimnilom. (Alma 23:8-13.) Opposition and conflict came from Amulon, Helam and Jerusalem. (Alma 24:1.) Jerusalem is the only one of these cities mentioned later in the Book of Mormon. At the time of the crucifixion, Jerusalem was covered by water. (3 Nephi 9:7.) Under Lake Atitlan, shown in figure 17, lies an ancient city from which divers have obtained numerous artifacts. Perhaps Jerusalem was covered by the lake which rose when the adjacent volcano erupted.

Shilom (near Nephi) and Shemlon could be seen from the tower at Nephi. Ishmael was "down" from Nephi. Middoni was "down" from Ishmael. Anti-Anti was "over" from Jerusalem, and also "over" from Middoni. Jerusalem joined the borders of Mormon. No other geographic information is available from the Book of Mormon for the land of Nephi and the surrounding cities and lands.

7

Lands Surrounding Zarahemla

City and Land of Zarahemla

More is written in the Book of Mormon about the city and the land of Zarahemla than about any other place. Zarahemla was the Nephite capital city, the center of political, social, religious, and military activity from the arrival of Mosiah about 200 B.C. until A.D. 34. When the crucifixion and terrible destruction occurred, Zarahemla was burned. (3 Nephi 8:8, 24; 9:3.) The city was rebuilt (4 Nephi 1:8), but rarely mentioned afterward. Only four verses of scripture refer to the city after it was destroyed. Bountiful became the center of activity. The temple in the land Bountiful was where the spiritual leaders were assembled when the resurrected Christ came in A.D. 34. (3 Nephi 11:1-11.)

Mosiah and a group of righteous Nephites found Zarahemla about 200 B.C. Mosiah had been "warned of the Lord that he should flee out of the land of Nephi." (Omni 1:12.) The Lord directed Mosiah in his journey from the city of Nephi, through the wilderness, and down into the land of Zarahemla. (Omni 1:13; see figure 18.)

figure 18

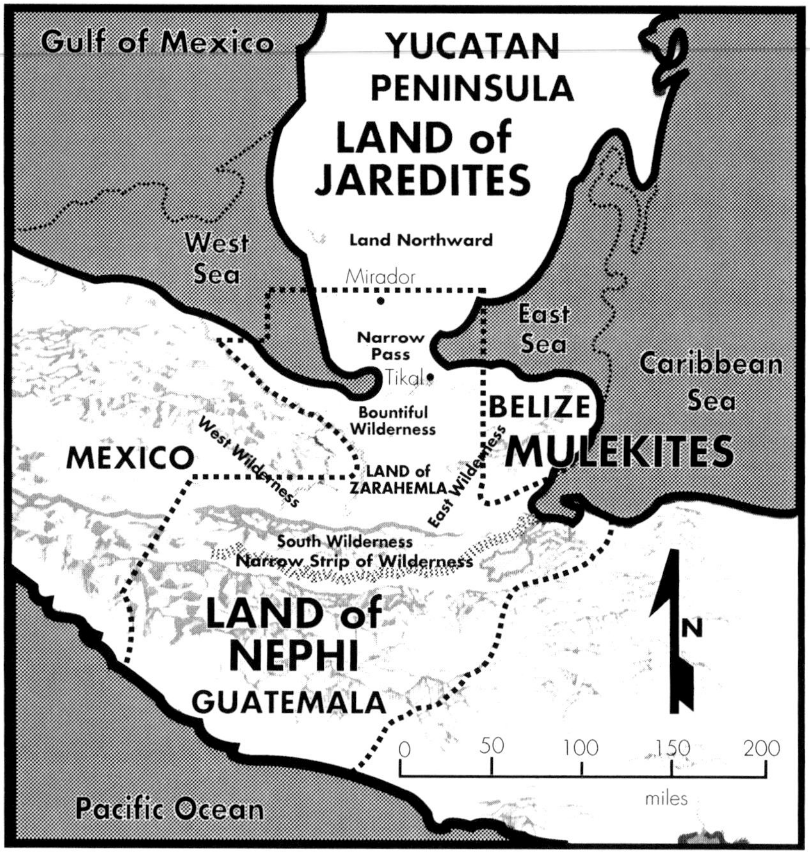

Land of Zarahemla and surrounding lands when Mosiah arrives in the city of Zarahemla about 200 B.C.

The leader Zarahemla and his people rejoiced, for they recognized that "the Lord had sent the people of

Mosiah with the plates of brass which contained the record of the Jews." (Omni 1:14.) "The people of Zarahemla, and of Mosiah, did unite together; and Mosiah was appointed to be their king." (Omni 1:19.) There were more of the people of Zarahemla than of the people of Mosiah (Mosiah 25:2), and there were more than twice as many Lamanites as there were people of Nephi and Zarahemla combined. (Mosiah 25:3.)

Cities and Lands Near and South of Zarahemla

The land of Zarahemla and surrounding lands when Mosiah arrived about 200 B.C. are shown in figure 18. The Sidon river is assumed to be the present-day Usumacinta river. The suggested general location for the cities and lands near Zarahemla is shown in figure 19.

figure 19

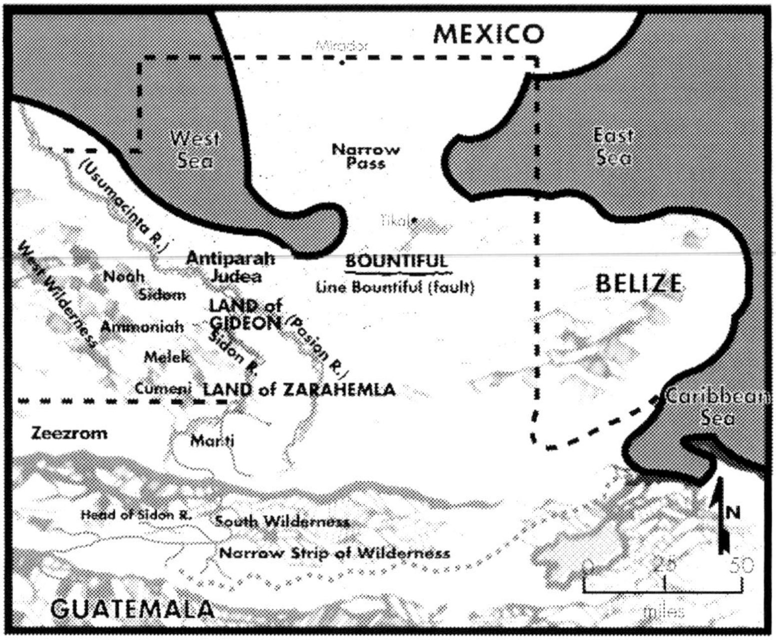

Cities and lands and the Sidon river in the land of Zarahemla.

The city of Zarahemla was toward the west side of the land occupied by the Nephites, and was on the west side of the Sidon river. (Alma 6:7.) The river was near Zarahemla, because many were baptized in the river. (Alma 4:4.) Headwaters of the Sidon river were in the south wilderness between Nephi and Zarahemla. The land of Gideon was on the east side of the Sidon river, perhaps a day's journey from Zarahemla. (Alma 2:15-20.) The land of Manti was north of the south wilderness (Alma 16:6), and was likely on the west side of the river. (Alma 43:32.)

Two hills near Zarahemla are mentioned. A hill Manti near Zarahemla, likely on the west side of the river, was where a man named Nehor "suffered an ignominious death" for killing the righteous Gideon. (Alma 1:9,15.) Across the Sidon river east from Zarahemla, a prominent hill Amnihu was the site of a furious battle between the Nephites and rebellious kingmen led by Amlici, another follower of Nehor. (Alma 2:1, 15-18.)

The defeated Amlicites fled south and met up with an army of Lamanites "in the land of Minon, above the land of Zarahemla, in the course of [on the road to] the land of Nephi." (Alma 2:24.) The Lamanite army was able to travel quickly from Minon to the vicinity of Zarahemla.

When the Nephite army, who had pitched their tents in the valley of Gideon, heard that a Lamanite army was approaching from the south and were then in the land of Minon, they rushed back to Zarahemla where they were attacked by the Lamanites as they were crossing to the west bank of the Sidon river. (Alma 2:27,34.) The Lamanites had come from Minon toward Zarahemla probably on the west side of the Sidon river. The land of Minon was likely south or southwest from Zarahemla, for when Alma journeyed southward from the land of Gideon toward the land of Manti, he did not mention Minon. (Alma 17:1.)

In what is here considered to be the valley of Gideon, eleven ancient ruins exist near the Pasion river in central Guatemala east of the Sidon (Usumacinta) river. Three of the eleven sites were occupied during Nephite times. South of the land of Manti in the south wilderness existed a prominent crossing of the river with a valley on the west and on the east side and a hill Riplah on the east side. (Alma 16:6-7; 43:27, 31-32, 35,41.) The Sidon river flowed northward from the south wilderness toward Zarahemla.

Cities Southwest from Zarahemla

Lamanite armies captured the cities of Manti, Zeezrom, and Cumeni about 63 B.C. (Alma 56:13-14.) After Antiparah in the north was liberated, the Nephites went southward and captured Cumeni. A counter-attacking Lamanite army was defeated and driven back to the city of Manti which they had captured earlier. (Alma 57:22.) Thus, Cumeni was probably northwest of Manti near the west wilderness.

Cities West and Northwest of Zarahemla

Mulek, Ammonihah, Aaron, and Sidom were visited by the prophet Alma. Antiparah was captured by the Lamanites. Judea was nearby but not captured, and Noah was approached by the Lamanite army after they destroyed Ammonihah. Their relative positions are shown in figure 19.

Antiparah was "in the borders by the seashore." (Alma 56:31.) Two scriptures have lead some authors to assume that Antiparah and hence Judea were on the Pacific coast of southern Mexico or Guatemala. Alma 53:8 states that Lamanite armies "on the west sea, south...obtained possession of a number of their [Nephite] cities in that part of the land." And Alma 53:22 states "that Helaman did march at the head of his 2000 stripling soldiers, to the support of the people [in the city Judea] in the borders of the land on the south by the west sea."

Insurmountable problems of logistics exist with the theory that Antiparah was on the Pacific coast. The nearby city of Judea was held by the Nephites, and reinforcements and supplies came without apparent difficulty from Zarahemla. (Alma 56:9, 15, 18, 57.) However, at least 150 miles separated the suggested location of Zarahemla from Judea (if Judea was on the Pacific coast), and the wilderness between would have been Lamanite territory. Many references in the Book of Mormon refer to a wilderness west of Zarahemla and between the city of Nephi and their first inheritance on the coast where they landed. Would the Nephites attempt to send rebellious prisoners to Zarahemla through 150 miles of Lamanite country? The entire history of the Nephites at Zarahemla describes activity relatively near their political and cultural center, not on the Pacific coast with at least 150 miles of Lamanite controlled wilderness between Zarahemla and Judea.

An alternative solution to the location of Judea lies in the Book of Mormon's reference to the west sea being at the narrow pass by the land Bountiful as discussed earlier. Refer to figure 19 as you consider that "west sea, south" (Alma 52:8) means the south coast of the west sea, and that "south by the west sea" (Alma 53:22) means land south of the west sea. Using these possibilities let us discuss the location of these cities northwest of Zarahemla.

In 82 B.C. Alma left his home in Zarahemla and journeyed "over into the land of Melek, on the west of the river Sidon, on the west by the borders of the wilderness." (Alma 8:1-3.) "When he had finished his work at Melek he departed thence, and traveled three days' journey on the north of the land of Melek; and he came to a city which was called Ammonihah." (Alma 8:6.)

The people of Ammonihah "would not hearkenen unto the words of Alma." (Alma 8:9.) The prophet prophesied that "except they repent the Lord God will destroy them." (Alma 8:16.) Alma left Ammonihah and traveled "towards the city which was called Aaron" (Alma 8:13), but the Lord directed him to return and give the people of Ammonihah a final warning. After that warning was given, Alma and Amulek, his missionary companion, departed out of the city of Ammonihah "and came out even into the land of Sidom; and behold, there they found all the people who had departed out of the land of Ammonihah, who had been cast out and stoned." (Alma 15:1.)

Within a year "the armies of the Lamanites had come in upon the wilderness side, into the borders of the land, even into the city of Ammonihah, and began to slay the people and destroy the city...and also some [people] around the borders of Noah." (Alma 16:2-3.) Recall that Lamanites were in, and came from, the wilderness west of Zarahemla.

Ten years later (72 B.C.), Lamanite armies again invaded, this time coming down out of the land of Nephi. Finding that Ammonihah had been strengthened and could not be captured, "they retreated into the wilderness...and marched toward the land of Noah." (Alma 49:12.) There they attacked the heavily fortified city of Noah and were defeated, fled into the wilderness, and returned to the land of Nephi. (Alma 49.)

Thus in summary, Melek was approximately west of Zarahemla near the wilderness, and Ammonihah was three days' journey north. Noah was not far from Ammonihah, likely northward since Alma did not mention Noah on his journey from Melek. Both Ammonihah and Noah were near the west wilderness. Sidom was probably east toward safer Nephite land, perhaps near the Sidon river. (See figure 19.)

About eight years later (about 64 B.C.), the Lamanites again attacked northwestern Nephite cities. Knowing that Ammonihah and Noah were heavily fortified, they attacked, conquered, and occupied Antiparah. (Alma 56:14.) By strategy, however, the Nephites were able to drive the Lamanites out, and the Lamanites "fled to their other cities, which they had possession of, to fortify them." (Alma 57:4.) The other cities are not mentioned and were likely further to the west or northwest, more in Lamanite territory from which the attack on Antiparah was probably launched.

The Nephite city of Judea was near Antiparah. (Alma 56:15, 18, 31, 33.) Helaman and his 2000 "sons" who were at Judea decoyed a strong Lamanite army out of Antiparah by marching nearby supposedly carrying supplies "to the city beyond, in the borders by the seashore." (Alma 56:30-31.) The Lamanite army pursued Helaman and his 2000 sons who fled northward for three days into the wilderness. (Alma 56:35-36, 40, 42.) The pursuing Lamanite army was defeated, Antiparah captured, and prisoners were sent to Zarahemla. (Alma 56:54, 57.) Helaman remained at Judea with his army to protect other Nephite "cities which were on the northward." (Alma 56:22.)

Judea was probably to the southeast of Antiparah. The retreat of Helaman's young warriors northward into the wilderness obviously did not take them through Lamanite territory. Judea was farther away from Lamanite strongholds than was Antiparah, because the Nephites were able to send their Lamanite prisoners to Zarahemla safely through Nephite country. These observations lend strong support for the opinion stated earlier, that Antiparah and Judea were not on the Pacific coast with at least 150 miles of Lamanite wilderness between them and Zarahemla.

That wilderness was west of Zarahemla is confirmed (1) by the stated location of Melek near the wilderness (Alma 8:3), (2) by the description of Lamanite land as recorded in Alma 22:27-28, and (3) by the account of defeated Lamanites fleeing from the vicinity of Zarahemla "towards the wilderness, which was west and north, away beyond the borders of the land;...until they reached the wilderness, which was called Hermounts." (Alma 2:35,57.)

Summary

Thus, Antiparah and Judea were probably northwest of Zarahemla, south of the west sea. Also Melek, Ammonihah, Noah, Aaron, and Sidom were more west of Zarahemla. Cumeni and Zeezrom were southwest of Zarahemla, and not far from Manti. (See figure 19.)

Apparently the Lamanite attacks came from the northwest and also from the southwest of Zarahemla. Melek lying west of Zarahemla was not attacked. It seems that an inhospitable wilderness was west of Zarahemla, perhaps the wilderness of Hermounts (Alma 2:37), and that Lamanite attacks came from the south and from the north ends of this wilderness of Hermounts (today known as the Lacandon homeland, and is still a wilderness).

8

Toward the Sea

East of Zarahemla

The land of Zarahemla, when discovered by Mosiah, was bounded by wilderness to the west, south, east, and north. (Alma 2:37; 8:3; 16:7; 22:29; 25:5,8; 31:3; 50:7,9; 62:34.) In 72 B.C., chief captain Moroni drove the Lamanites out of the east wilderness, colonized the area, and fortified the "borders of the seashore" between Nephites and Lamanites. (Alma 50:7, 9-10.)

Alma and Helaman recorded much detail concerning the location of eleven cities east of Zarahemla toward the sea east. Nine of these cities listed from north to south are near the sea: Mulek, Jershon, Gid, Omner, Morianton, Lehi, Moroni, Antionum, and Siron. Two cities are inland (Aaron and Nephihah), both were west of Morianton, Lehi, and Moroni. Throughout Mormon's record, he consistently lists cities in the order of their location. Figure 20 shows the suggested relative location of these cities near the Caribbean Sea.

figure 20

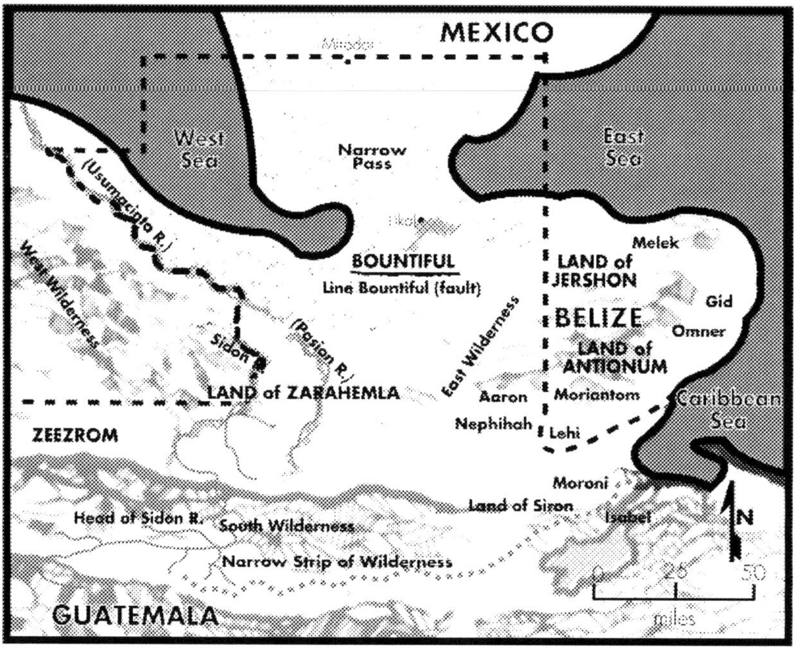

Cities and lands east of Zarahemla near the Caribbean Sea.

The first city built in the area was Moroni "by the east sea; and it was south by the line of the possessions of the Lamanites." (Alma 50:13.) A wilderness existed on the south and east at Moroni. (Alma 63:34.) Nephihah and the plains of Nephihah (Alma 62:18) were between Moroni and Aaron. (Alma 50:14.) (Another city called Aaron was west of Zarahemla near Ammonihah; see Alma 8:13.)

Moriantun was north of Moroni, with Lehi between, both on the borders by the seashore. (Alma 50:25.) Then came the cities of Omner, Gid, and Mulek, all by the seashore. (Alma 51:26.) The land of Jershon was on the east by the sea, south of the land Bountiful. (Alma 27:22.)

"Zoramites had gathered themselves together in a land which they called Antionum, which was east of the land of Zarahemla, which lay nearly bordering upon the seashore, which was south of the land of Jershon, which also bordered upon the wilderness south, which wilderness was full of Lamanites." (Alma 31:3.) Apparently the land of Siron where the harlot Isabel lived (Alma 39:2-3) was south of Antionum.

City of Mulek

The city of Mulek was "on the east borders by the seashore." (Alma 51:26.) The heavily fortified city of Bountiful was the closest major city to Mulek, and plains existed between the two cities. (Alma 52:20.) A wilderness was west of the city of Mulek. (Alma 52:22.)

The city of Mulek is here assumed to be the initial land of the Mulekites. Confirmation is circumstantial, but several statements and conditions support the assumption.

1. The name "Mulek" is significant, because Mormon states, and the written record confirms, that cities and villages were named after their founder. (Alma 8:7.) For example the city of Nephi and the city of Zarahemla were named after their founders Nephi and Zarahemla. (2 Nephi 5:8; Mosiah 25:2.)

2. The people of Mulek lived in the land of their first inheritance for approximately 300 to 400 years, contemporary with both the Jaredites and the Nephites without apparently having much, if any, knowledge of each other.

3. The people of Zarahemla left the land of their first of inheritance which was the land of Mulek, came up into the wilderness, and founded the city of Zarahemla. (Omni 1:15-16.)

4. A reasonable location for the land and city of Mulek is east or southeast of the land and city of Bountiful in the present country of Belize. Mulekites living in Belize would have been separated from Jaredites living in the Yucatan by a wilderness, by much water on the north, and by a narrow pass. Nephites before Mosiah's time would have been separated from Mulekites in Belize by wilderness and the narrow strip of wilderness.

5. Archaeologists have found numerous ancient sites and structures in Belize.

9

The Narrow Pass, Bountiful, Hagoth, and Cumorah

Mormon's abridgement of the writings of Alma and other prophets who referred to the narrow pass, Bountiful, and Hagoth are vital to confirming the location of Book of Mormon lands. These features were discussed briefly in Chapter 3 as an overview and as a reference for the more detailed discussion which followed. However, the importance of the pass, Bountiful, and Hagoth is the reason for some duplication and a more detailed discussion in this chapter.

The Narrow Pass

The most distinctive physical feature in the Book of Mormon was the narrow pass, also called a passage or neck. A sea existed to the west and to the east of the pass before the crucifixion. A land the Nephites called Desolation (the land of the Jaredites) was north of the pass. Bountiful was south of the pass. (Alma 22:31-33; 50:34; 52:9; 63:5.) Seas west and east of the narrow pass are mentioned frequently by Alma between 90 and 55 B.C.

Authors attempting to locate Book of Mormon lands have been frustrated because no existing geographical feature like a narrow pass fits the written record. Some earlier authors suggested that the Panama Canal area between North and South America is the pass spoken of in the Book of Mormon. This assumption has lead to the unsubstantiated and discarded claim that Zarahemla was in South America and Cumorah was in upper New York State, thousands of miles away. Other authors have suggested the Isthmus of Tehuantepec in Central Mexico as the pass. (See figure 1.) Both locations (Panama and Tehuantepec) have seas to the north and south, not west and east. Another author suggests the Pacific coastal corridor in lower Mexico below Tehuantepec, but mountains, not a sea, exists east of the coastal corridor. Also this coastal corridor is oriented northwest-to-southeast (see figure 1), whereas the narrow pass has a north-south orientation in the written record. Other adjacent geographical features to the north and south of the narrow pass, clearly noted in the Book of Mormon, do not exist at the suggested locations.

Several researchers have called attention to the following statement in 3 Nephi 8:11-12 describing destruction and physical changes that occurred when Christ was crucified. "And there was a great and terrible destruction in the land southward. But behold, there was a more great and terrible destruction in the land northward; for behold, the whole face of the land was changed." (3 Nephi 8:13.) At the sites suggested by some authors for the narrow pass (Panama, Isthmus of Tehuantepec, Pacific coastal corridor) physical evidence does not exist that "the whole face of the land was changed."

In chapter 3, I made the very basic and major assumption that before the crucifixion two drainage basins, one west and one east of Tikal, were the seas west and east of the narrow pass. (See figure 6.) The following discussion based upon the written record will show that this assumption is worthy of serious consideration.

A study of maps of Guatemala showing topography and ancient dwelling sites also support the suggestion that the narrow pass (or passage or neck) was on the higher ground where Tikal and Mirador are located. Extensive ruins exist north and south from this location, which indicates a major north-south trade route.

The over-thrusting of the tectonic plates at the narrow strip of wilderness in central Guatemala, discussed in chapter 3 and shown in figure 3, quite likely resulted in a rise in elevation of northern Guatemala and the Yucatan Peninsula changing "the whole face of the land." Thus, the west and east seas may have drained and became the existing marshy areas and drainages that are now west and east of Tikal.

figure 21

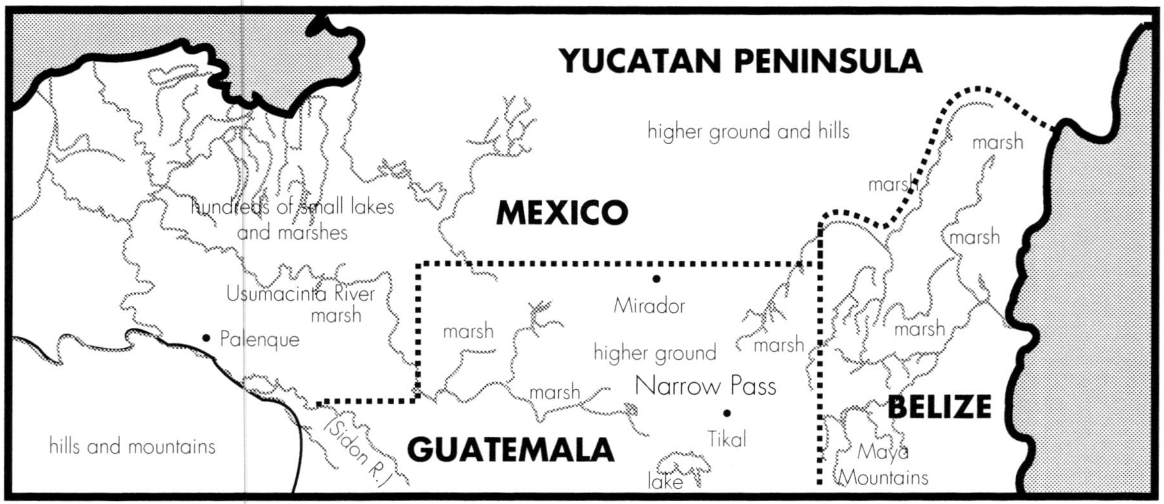

Vicinity of the Narrow Pass today. A simplified drawing of an aerial flight map (ONC J-25).

Figure 21 is a simplified drawing made from an aerial flight map (ONC J-25) that I used while flying over Guatemala and Mexico. Shown are the existing Yucatan Peninsula, Guatemala, and Belize. Major west and east river systems with many lakes, marshes and tributaries exist near northern Guatemala. The present drainage east of Tikal also contains marshes but has a more pronounced drainage system than the area west of Tikal. Before the crucifixion, the area outlined as the east sea in prior figures undoubtedly contained more promontories into the sea than did the area outlined as the west sea. An extensive marsh now extends for 70 miles west from Tikal. Farther northwest is the meandering outlet of the Ucamacinta River with many small lakes and marshes, a nearly uninhabited marshland. The assumed location of the narrow pass is the watershed between the west and east rivers near Tikal and Mirador.

Higher Ground and Hills

The 500-foot contour showing higher elevations in the southern Yucatan is outlined in figure 22. A strip of land and several hills above 500 feet elevation lie north of the assumed narrow pass. Is it possible that the Jaredite city of Moron and also the hills Shem and Cumorah (Ramah) are located on this higher ground north of Tikal? The central elongated hill in the center of the 500 feet contour rises to a height of 1017 feet above sea level, approximately 500 feet above the surrounding land.

Robison states that the nearby city of Becan, shown in figure 22, "was unique in the classical Maya period because it was a fortified city. Its inner core was surrounded by an immense dry moat which averaged 17 feet deep by 50 wide. The excavated earthen material formed a high bulwark on the inward side of the moat." (The Maya Legacy, Stanford Robison, Map, 1977.) Perhaps Becan was an ancient Nephite city near Cumorah.

figure 22

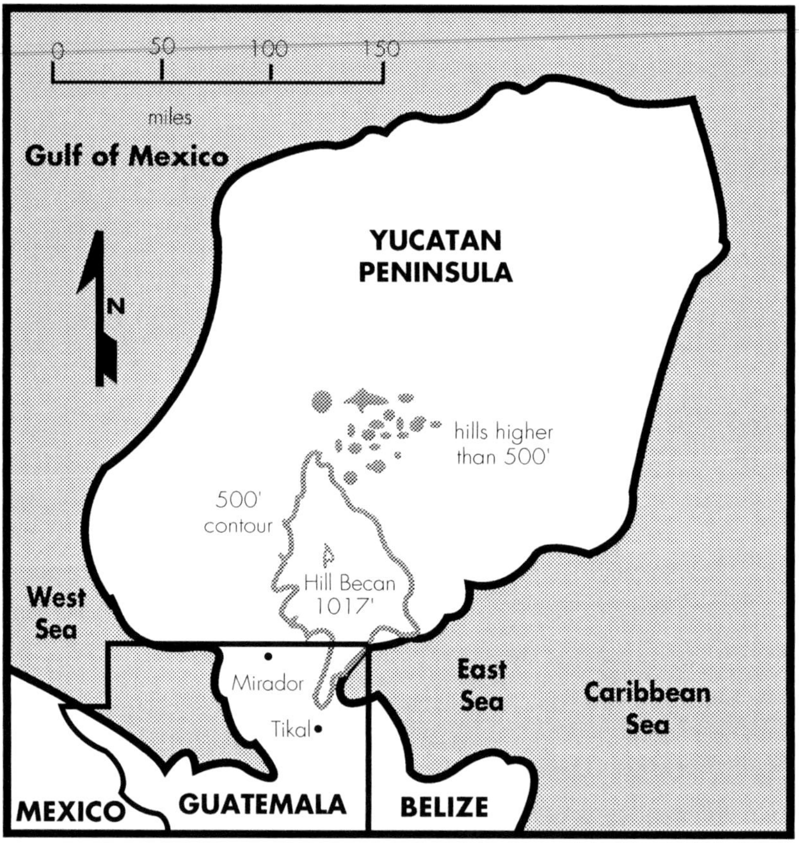

Possible location of hill Shim and Cumorah (Ramah) on higher ground above 500 feet in the centeral Yucatan Peninsula, north of the assumed location of the Narrow Pass near Tikal.

The Line Bountiful

Robison also called attention to a fault escarpment about 60 miles long running from west to east and just north of Flores and lake Peten Itza. While in Guatemala recently, I obtained detailed geologic maps (*Mapa, Geologico de la Republica de Guatemala*) which show the 60 mile fault near Flores, with another 20 miles of fault inferred to the east. (Figure 23.)

figure 23

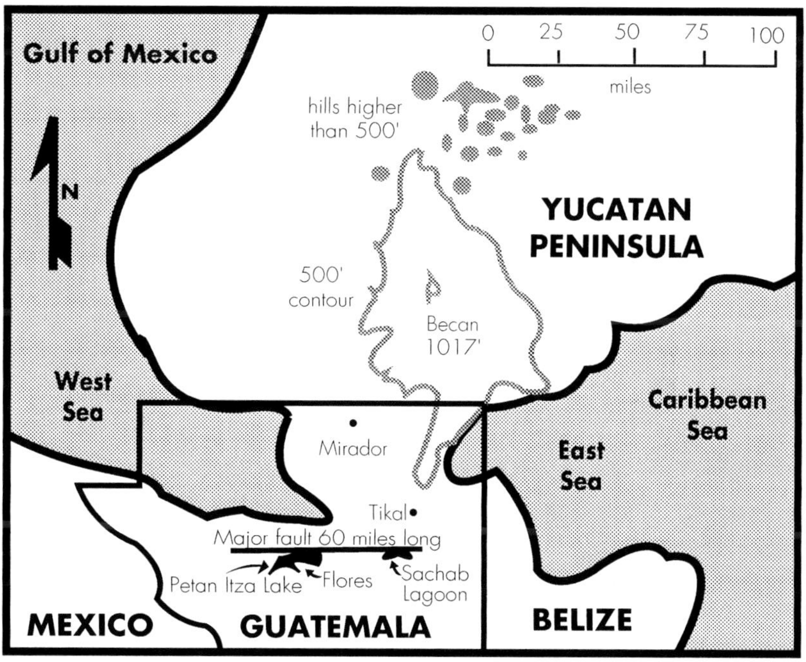

The Line Bountiful, a long east-west fault in northern Guatemala south of Tikal.

This prominent fault might explain the following perplexing statement about the "line Bountiful." "And now, it was only the distance of a day and a half's journey for a Nephite, on the line Bountiful and the land Desolation, from the east to the west sea; and thus the land of Nephi and the land of Zarahemla were nearly surrounded by water, their being a small neck of land between the land northward [the land Desolation of the Jaredites] and the land southward" [the land Bountiful]. (Alma 22:32.) The land of Bountiful has been shown to be south of the land Desolation. Assuming that the fault escarpment shown in figure 23 was the "line Bountiful" permits several significant statements to be made.

1. The narrow pass is north of and adjacent to the line Bountiful.

2. A west sea and an east sea existed before the crucifixion near and north of the line Bountiful.

3. The city Bountiful was near the line Bountiful.

4. The prominent and major ancient cities of Tikal and Mirador were in the vicinity of the land of the Jaredites and the land Bountiful.

Bountiful

"The land on the northward [northward of the narrow pass] was called Desolation [by the Nephites], and the land on the southward was called Bountiful, it being the wilderness which is filled with all manner of wild animals of every kind, a part of which had come from the land northward for food." (Alma 22:31.) Thus, the land both south and north of the line Bountiful was a wilderness until colonized by the Nephites about 70 B.C.

This statement by Alma referring to a wilderness called Bountiful was made between 90 and 77 B.C. The first mention of the city Bountiful was in 65 B.C. (Alma 52:17.) The land Bountiful was colonized and a city established about 71 B.C., when chief captain Moroni colonized lands east of Zarahemla near the sea to block Lamanite movement northward from the narrow strip of wilderness. In fact most references to Bountiful after 65 B.C. deal with efforts to block Lamanite armies from gaining access to the land northward. (Alma 51:30-32; 52:17-18; 53:3-4; Helaman 1:23,29.)

In 55 B.C. "There was a large company of men, even to the amount of five thousand and four hundred men, with their wives and their children [likely more than 10,000 people], departed out of the land of Zarahemla into the land which was northward." (Alma 63:4.) In 46 B.C. "an exceedingly great many who departed out of the land of Zarahemla, and went forth into the land northward to inherit the land." (Helaman 3:3.)

After civil conflict had driven the more righteous Nephites to Bountiful, the city of Zarahemla was destroyed by fire when Christ was crucified. (3 Nephi 9:3.) Thus, Bountiful became the center of religious and civil leadership. (See figure 18.) The most important reference to the land Bountiful was the appearance of the resurrected Christ to the temple where the leadership of the church and those to be called as special disciples were assembled. They were likely in conference in the month of April, a year after Christ's resurrection reporting on conditions following extensive destruction that had occurred at the time of the crucifixion. (3 Nephi 11:1-10.)

Hagoth

Much has been written about Hagoth sailing into the west sea, assumed by some writers to be the Pacific Ocean, and suggesting that Hagoth was the ancestor of the Polynesian people. Therefore, a careful review of the scriptures concerning Hagoth is important.

In the same year that "a large company of men...with their wives and children departed out of the land of Zarahemla into the land northward" (Alma 63:4), Hagoth "went forth and built him an exceedingly large ship, on the borders of the land Bountiful, by the land Desolation, and launched it forth into the west sea, by the narrow neck which led into the land northward." (Alma 63:5.)

These two verses clearly and unmistakable identify the location of the launching, by specifically mentioning Bountiful, Desolation, west sea, narrow neck (pass) and land northward. If the narrow neck was where I believe it was, Hagoth sailed northward into the Gulf of Mexico, not westward into the Pacific Ocean.

The next verse is also enlightening in that "there were many of the Nephites who did enter therein [into Hagoth's ship] and did sail forth with much provisions, and also many women and children; and they took their course northward." (Alma 63:6.)

Again significant statements are made; many families entered, with much provisions, and they sailed northward, not westward. They obviously knew where they were going, and they intended to colonize a land northward.

The following verse states that in the year following 54 B.C., "this man [Hagoth] built other ships. And the first ship did also return, and many more people did enter into it; and they also took much provisions, and set out again to the land northward." (Alma 63:7.)

Note that the first ship returned, and many more people with much provision again went to the land northward. There was no hesitancy. Those who sailed first and those who went in the same ship the following year knew where they were going. They knew the land northward. This land northward was not an unknown land far away in the western Pacific as some have assumed. Even though the first ship did not return from the second trip, without apparent hesitation another ship sailed forth. (Alma 63:8.)

The risen, resurrected Jesus came 89 years later at A.D. 34, and 200 golden years followed. Commerce and shipping would have been extensive. More Nephites undoubtedly went to the land northward, and other Nephites could have and probably did go to the western Pacific and to the Polynesian islands. Prophetic statements and patriarchal blessings have confirmed that many of the Polynesians are descendants of the Nephites.

Since Hagoth is the only person mentioned in the Book of Mormon who sailed forth, his name has become synonymous with Nephites who sailed into the Pacific. However, if I am correct, Hagoth sailed from the Yucatan northward into the Gulf of Mexico. Increasing evidence suggests that Jaredites may have also gone to the land northward, to the Mississippi and Ohio basins, and left a legacy as "the mound builders" about 800 B.C., but that is another story. Numerous publications present evidence of Jaredite and later Nephite influence among North American Indians. One who reviewed a draft copy of this book made an interesting comment; "This brings Nephite blood closer to home."

Cumorah—Land of Many Waters, Rivers, and Fountains

Mormon in describing the retreat of the Nephite army states that "it came to pass that we did march forth to the land of Cumorah, and we did pitch our tents around the hill Cumorah; and it was in a land of many waters, rivers, and fountains." (Mormon 6:4.) Nearly a thousand years earlier, Nephi made an interesting statement after they had traveled in the Arabian wilderness for eight years. "And we beheld the sea, which we called Irreantum, which, being interpreted, is many waters." (1 Nephi 17:5.) In numerous scriptures Nephi is clearly referring to the sea/ocean when he writes about "many waters." (1 Nephi 13:10, 12-13, 29; 14:11-12.) Moroni when abridging the record of the Jaredites also refers to the sea as "many waters." (Ether 2:6; 6:7.)

If the land of the Jaredites hill Ramah, which is the Nephite hill Cumorah, is on the Yucatan Peninsula, this land is truly in the language of the Book of Mormon a land of "many waters". This land is surrounded by seas, and it has "many rivers and fountains." Some rivers reach the sea, but many sink into the heavily fractured limestone and reappear as springs. The central Yucatan Peninsula is a broad rather flat plain with few established drainages. Thus, the suggested land of the Jaredites in the

Yucatan, the land northward of the narrow pass, does have many waters, streams, and fountains.

10

Destruction of the Nephites

Battles for Survival

For two hundred years following the ministry of the resurrected Christ, the righteous descendants of father Lehi experienced a golden era. But by A.D. 300 major wars between Nephites and Lamanites were occurring. In A.D. 327-328, Mormon, a fifteen-year-old lad, was appointed leader of Nephite armies. (Mormon 1:15; 2:1-2.) For 58 years he led the Nephites, and admonished them to be more righteous.

The record says that Mormon "was large in stature," both physically and spiritually. He himself states that he was "somewhat of a sober mind, therefore I was visited of the Lord, and tasted and knew of the goodness of Jesus." (Mormon 1:15.)

The locations of the battles for the nearly 60 years from A.D. 327 to 385 add some clarity and tend to confirm the assumed location of Book of Mormon lands. During the following discussion, refer to figure 24.

figure 24

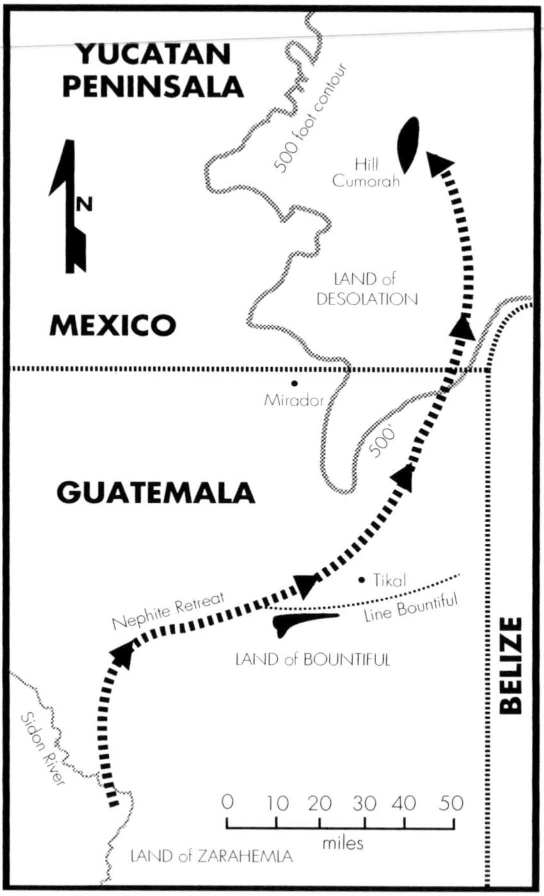

Retreat of Nephite armies northward from Zarahemla to the south side of the West Sea, and then to the Land of Desolation where the final battle occurred by the Hill Cumorah in the Yucatan Peninsula.

Battles began "in the borders of Zarahemla, by the waters of Sidon." (Mormon 1:10.) Nephites retreated toward the north countries (Mormon 2:3), then to the city of Angola, to the land of David, and to the land of Joshua "which was in the borders west by the seashore." (Mormon 2:3-6.) This retreat northward likely would be from Zarahemla to the south shore of the west sea. These were major all-out battles, for the Lamanites had an army of 44,000, and the Nephites had 42,000. (Mormon 2:9.) This series of conflicts occupied 19 years (A.D. 326 to 345.)

The Nephites then retreated to the city of Jashon which "was near the land [Shem] where Ammaron had deposited the records [in the hill Shim]. And behold I [Mormon] had gone according to the word of Ammaron, and taken the plates of Nephi." (Mormon 2:17.) Mormon was now about 24 years old.

The Nephites were next driven "northward to the land which was called Shem" where they fought with an army of 30,000 against a Lamanite army of 50,000. (Mormon 2:20,25.) The Nephites were losing both ground and men.

In A.D. 350 the Nephites "made a treaty with the Lamanites and the robbers of Gadianton, in which we did get the lands of our inheritance divided. And the Lamanites did give unto us the land northward, yea, even to the narrow passage which led into the land southward. And we did give unto the Lamanites all land southward." (Mormon 2:28-29.) Thus, the Nephites were now given the land north of the narrow passage.

Ten years later (A.D. 360), Lamanites attacked Nephites at the city Desolation "which was in the borders, [north of and] by the narrow pass which led into the land southward." Nephites beat the Lamanites twice "and did slay a great number of them, and their dead were cast into the sea." (Mormon 3:5-8.) As shown in figure 21, the prominent seas west and east had been replaced in Mormons time with extensive marshes and tributaries. If the city Desolation was on higher ground near the narrow pass, the drainage to the east contains more distinct streams capable of carrying dead to the sea. Several ancient cities existed within the east drainage after the crucifixion.

Note the clear references thus far to the sea, the narrow passage or pass, the land northward, and the land southward. These scriptures fit well the suggested location of Book of Mormon lands.

Despite their victories, the Nephites were unrepentant, and in A.D. 363 Mormon refused to lead them. (Mormon 3:11-12.) The Nephite army went up out of Desolation, which was near the sea, to attack the Lamanites and were defeated. The Nephites then lost the city Desolation, and fled to the nearby city Teancum that "lay in the borders by the seashore." (Mormon 4:2-3.) Several battles occurred and finally both Desolation and Teancum were lost. Nephites then fled to the city Boaz, and it was lost. (Mormon 4:1-21.)

"And now I, Mormon, seeing that the Lamanites were about to overthrow the land, therefore I did go to the hill Shim, and did take up all the records which Ammaron had hid up unto the Lord." (Mormon 4:23.)

Mormon moved these records to the hill Cumorah (Mormon 6:6), which was probably northward of the hill Shim, since the Lamanites were driving from the south.

Seeing the desperate condition of the Nephites, Mormon repented of the oath which he had made some 10 years earlier and again took command of the army, at the advanced age of 64. At Jordan and at other nearby strongholds, the Nephites cut off the Lamanites so they "could not get into the country which lay before us, to destroy the inhabitants of the land." (Mormon 5:1-4.) Jordan and the other strongholds must have been near the narrow pass. Five years later (in A.D. 380) Jordan was over-run and only "those whose flight was swifter than the Lamanites did escape." (Mormon 5:7.)

The Nephites were facing annihilation. Mormon wrote a letter to the king of the Lamanites and obtained permission to "gather together our people unto the land of Cumorah, by a hill which was called Cumorah, and there we could give them battle...and it was in a land of many waters, rivers, and fountains." (Mormon 6:2,4.)

The locations of the cities mentioned in the Nephite retreat from Zarahemla until their defeat at Cumorah are not well defined, but figure 24 shows the suggested general route of their retreat based upon all of the scriptural evidence noted so far in this document. The Nephite retreat likely took them eastward past Bountiful into the area were major streams emptied into the sea. Recall that at Desolation, which was in the borders by the narrow pass, Lamanite dead had been cast into the sea. (Mormon 3:5,8; 4:3.)

"I, Mormon, began to be old [an understandable statement at age 73]; and knowing it to be the last struggle of my people, ...therefore I made this record out of the plates of Nephi, and hid up in the hill Cumorah all the records which had been entrusted to me by the hand of the Lord, save it were these few plates which I gave unto my son Moroni." (Mormon 6:6.)

Thus, in my view, the hill Cumorah must be in the Yucatan Peninsula north of the narrow pass. Figure 23 shows the 500 feet contours in this portion of the Yucatan. Several hills exist which could be candidates for the hill Shim and the hill Cumorah.

The Refugee Moroni

The final Nephite battle near the hill Cumorah occurred about A.D. 385. Killed were 230,000 fighting men plus women and children and aged, likely a million Nephites. (Mormon 6:10-15.) Only 24 survived. (Mormon 6:11.) After sixteen years (A.D. 401) Moroni was able to slip back undetected to where his father had deposited the Nephite records. He had been a hunted refugee for 16 long years. (Mormon 8:2-5.)

"Behold I, Moroni, do finish the record of my father, Mormon. Behold, I have but few things to write, which things I have been commanded by my father. And now it came to pass that after the great and tremendous battle at Cumorah, behold, the Nephites who had escaped into the country southward were hunted by the Lamanites, until they were all destroyed. And my father also was killed by them, and I even remain alone to write the sad tale of the destruction of my people. But behold, they are gone, and I fulfil the commandments of my father. And whether they will slay me, I know not. Therefore I will write and hide up the records in the earth; and whither I go it mattereth not. Behold, my father hath made this record, and he hath written the intent thereof. And behold, I would write it also if I had room upon the plates, but I have not; and ore I have none, for I am alone. My father hath been slain in battle, and all my kinsfolk, and I have not friends nor whither to go; and how long the Lord will suffer that I may live I know not." (Mormon 8:1-5.)

Sometime between A.D. 401 and 421, the refugee Moroni obtained some ore and was able to make an abridgment of the account of the people of Jared, the Book of Ether, and to write other very important information. Moroni states that " I had supposed not to have written more, but I have not as yet perished; and I make not myself known to the Lamanites lest they should destroy me. For behold, their wars are exceedingly fierce among themselves; and because of their hatred they put to death every Nephite that will not deny the Christ. And I, Moroni, will not deny the Christ; wherefore, I wander whithersoever I can for the safety of mine own life." (Moroni 1:1-3.)

By A.D. 421, the record known today as the Book of Mormon was completed and deposited in upper New York state. Moroni had been a refugee for a long 36 years. Moroni's life was preserved for a wise purpose, to eventually deposit the Nephite record in a hill, thousands of miles away from his homeland. The Book of Mormon was deposited in a hill in upper New York State where Joseph Smith would be living 1,400 years later.

Moroni accomplished much in his lifetime. He remained true to the faith, and gave to us the Book of Mormon, written for us that we might better prepare for the return of the Savior.

Book of Mormon Land

And thus the written record contains many valuable clues pertaining to Book of Mormon lands. When all of these clues are applied to the lands of Guatemala, Belize and Yucatan Peninsula, a consistent and seemly logical pattern emerges. The suggested location adds clarity to our understanding and our testimony. Our primary source of information must be the Book of Mormon "the most correct book of any book on earth."

As I stated early in this book, my sincere hope is that some ideas I have presented will be of value to those who, with a sincere heart and with real intent, are seeking to better understand where Book of Mormon people lived, and thereby to draw closer to them and to obtain a greater love for their sacred record and for their Savior and our Savior, Jesus the Christ.